The LEGO® Christmas Ornaments Book

• 15 DESIGNS TO SPREAD HOLIDAY CHEER •

CHRIS MCVEIGH

No Starch Press
San Francisco

Printed in China

First printing

20 19 18 17 16   1 2 3 4 5 6 7 8 9

ISBN-10: 1-59327-766-0
ISBN-13: 978-1-59327-766-6

Publisher: William Pollock
Production Editor: Serena Yang
Cover Design: Beth Middleworth
Developmental Editor: Tyler Ortman
Compositor: Serena Yang
Proofreader: Emelie Burnette

For information on distribution, translations, or bulk sales, please contact No Starch Press, Inc. directly:

No Starch Press, Inc.
245 8th Street, San Francisco, CA 94103
phone: 415.863.9900; info@nostarch.com; www.nostarch.com

Library of Congress Cataloging-in-Publication Data:

Names: McVeigh, Chris (Artist) author.
Title: The LEGO Christmas ornaments book / by Chris McVeigh.
Description: San Francisco : No Starch Press, [2016]
Identifiers: LCCN 2016003449| ISBN 9781593277666 | ISBN 1593277660
Subjects: LCSH: Christmas tree ornaments. | LEGO toys.
Classification: LCC TT900.C4 M38 2016 | DDC 745.594/12--dc23
LC record available at http://lccn.loc.gov/2016003449

Production Date: 5/23/16
Plant & Location: Printed by Everbest Printing (Guangzhou, China), Co. Ltd
Job / Batch #: 66417-0 / 803151 R3

To Iris, for the confidence;
to Irene, for the creativity;
and to Frances, for the courage

Contents

Introduction

Christmas and LEGO were always very special to me as a child, and so as an adult, it's been great fun to combine the two. I hope you and your family enjoy building these bold, bright ornaments and hanging them from your tree. And remember to mix it up—swap colors, switch parts, and put your own spin on them!

You can find more ornament designs at my site: *chrismcveigh.com*.

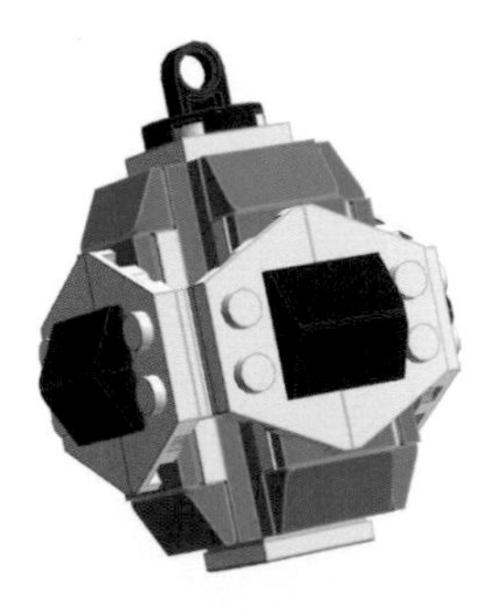

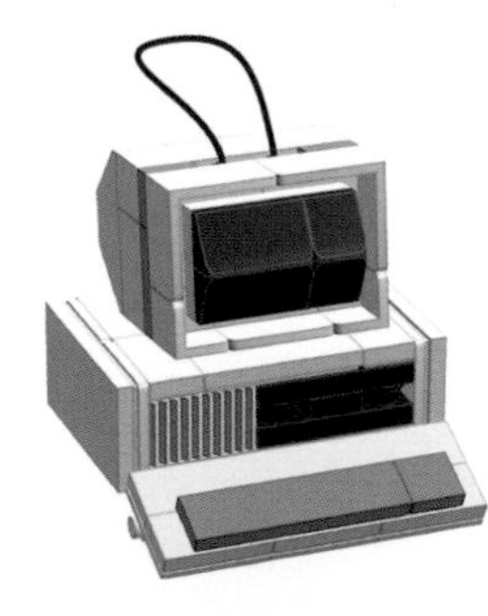

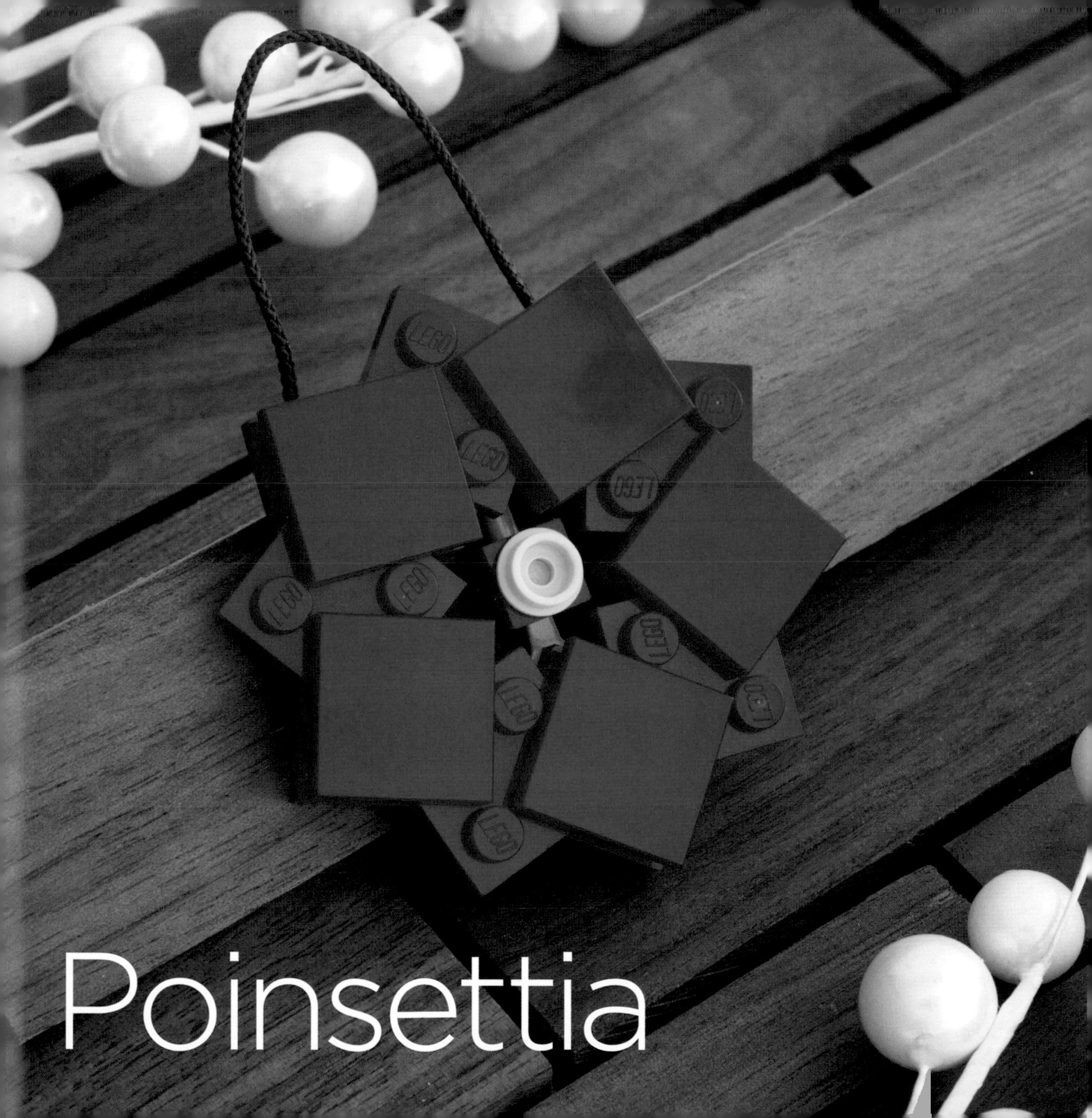

Poinsettia

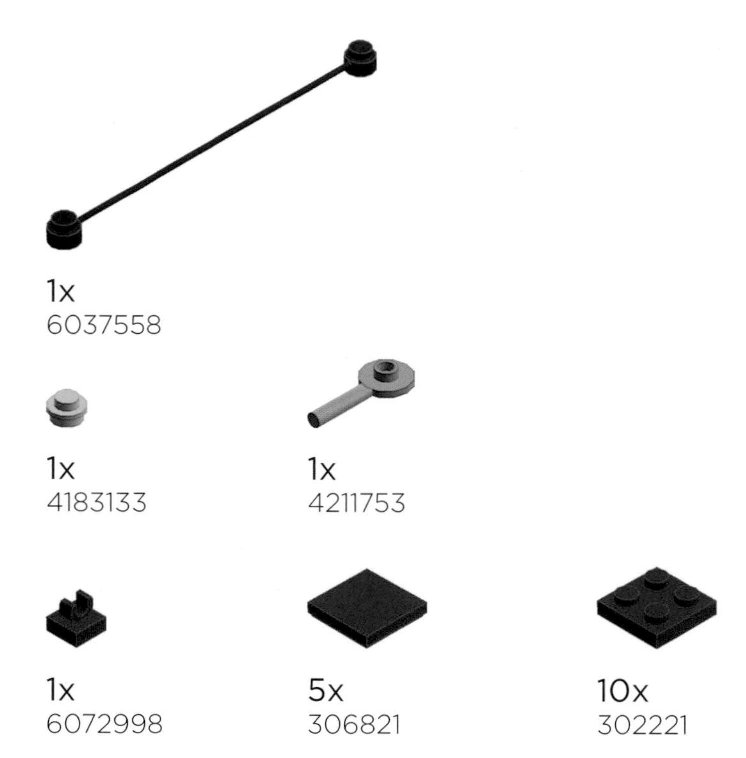
1x
6037558
1x
4183133
1x
4211753
1x
6072998
5x
306821
10x
302221

1

2

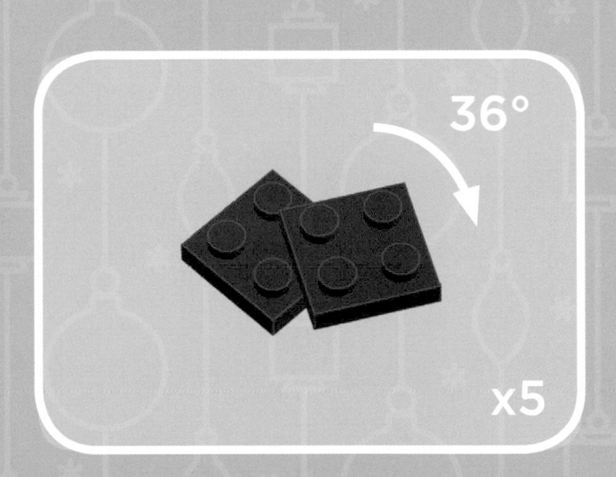

3

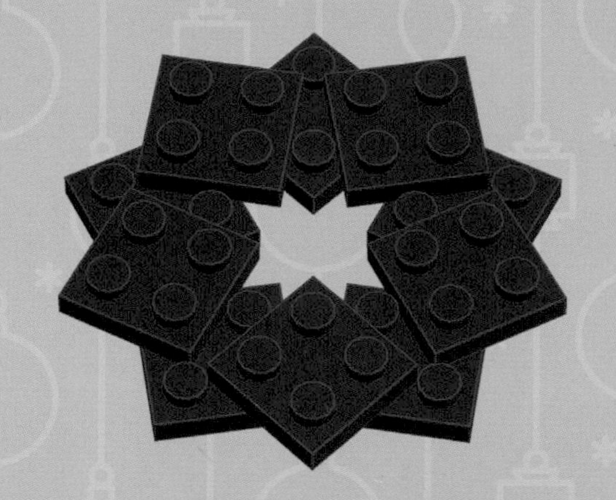

5

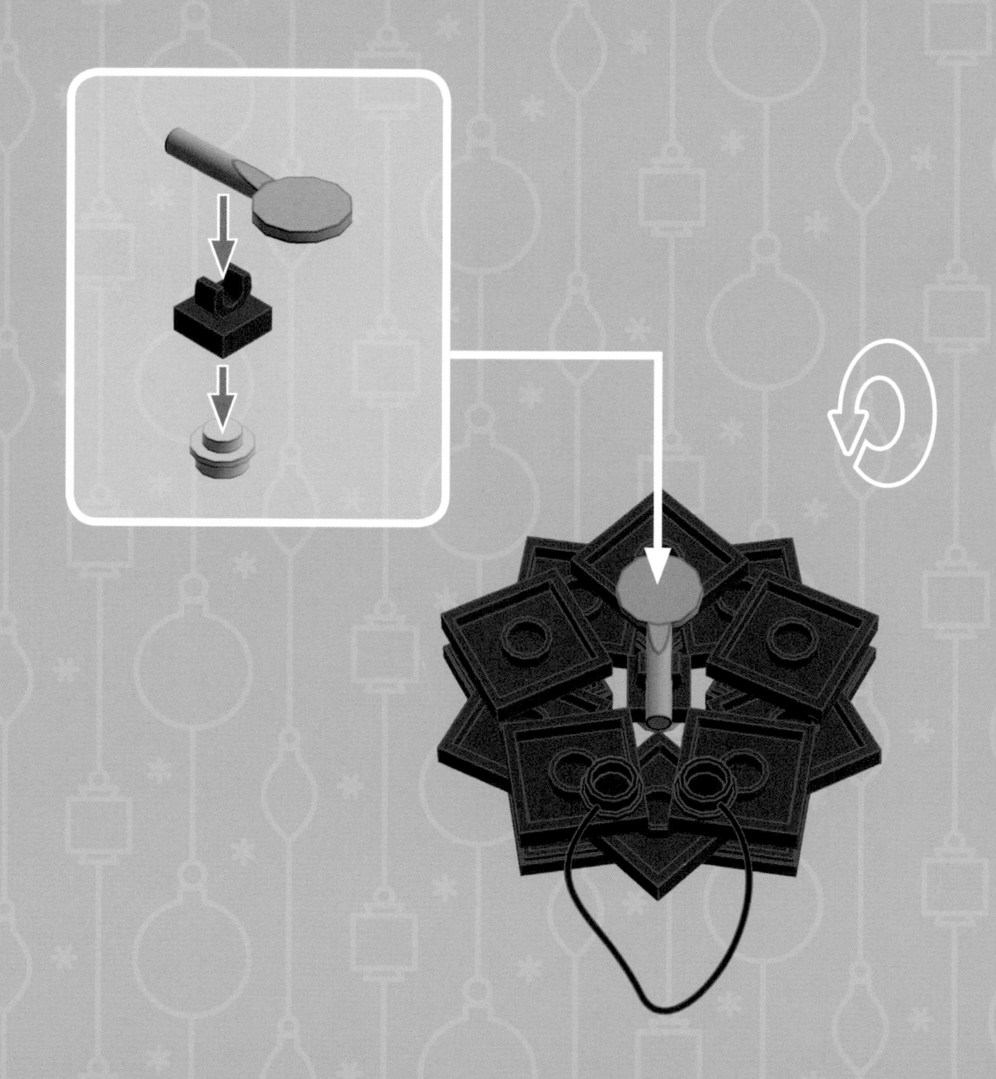

Snowflake

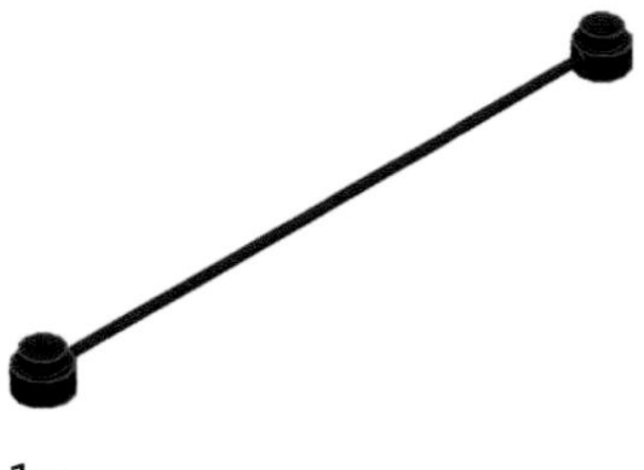

1x
6037558

6x
403201

6x
242001

6x
302201

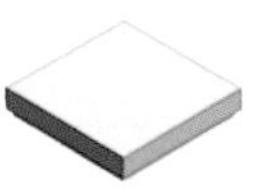

6x
306801

1

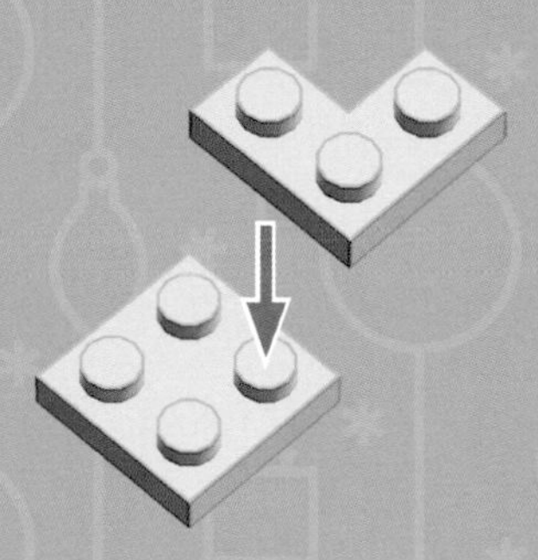

2

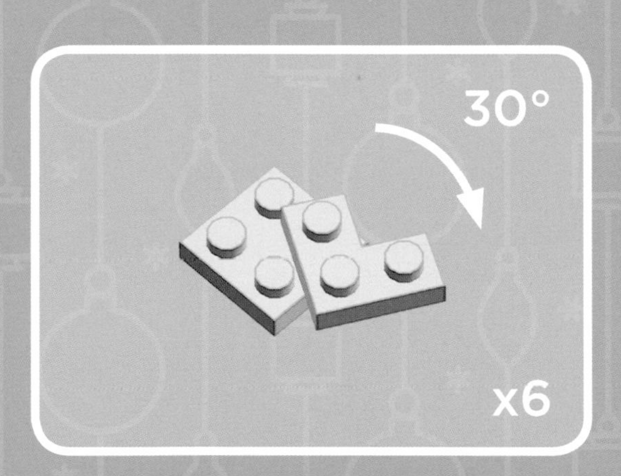

3

4

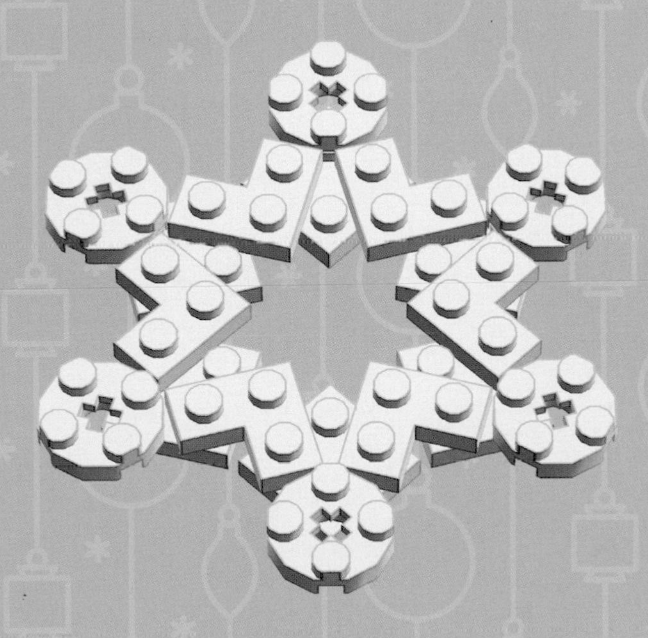

5

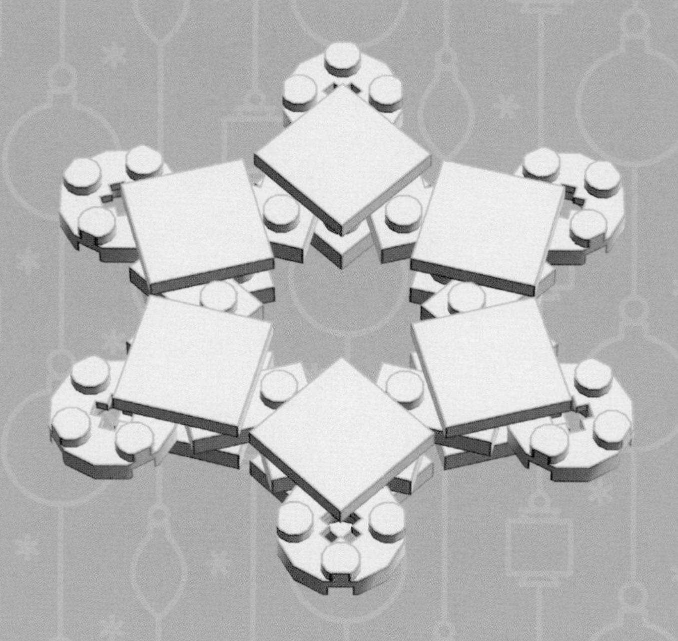

6

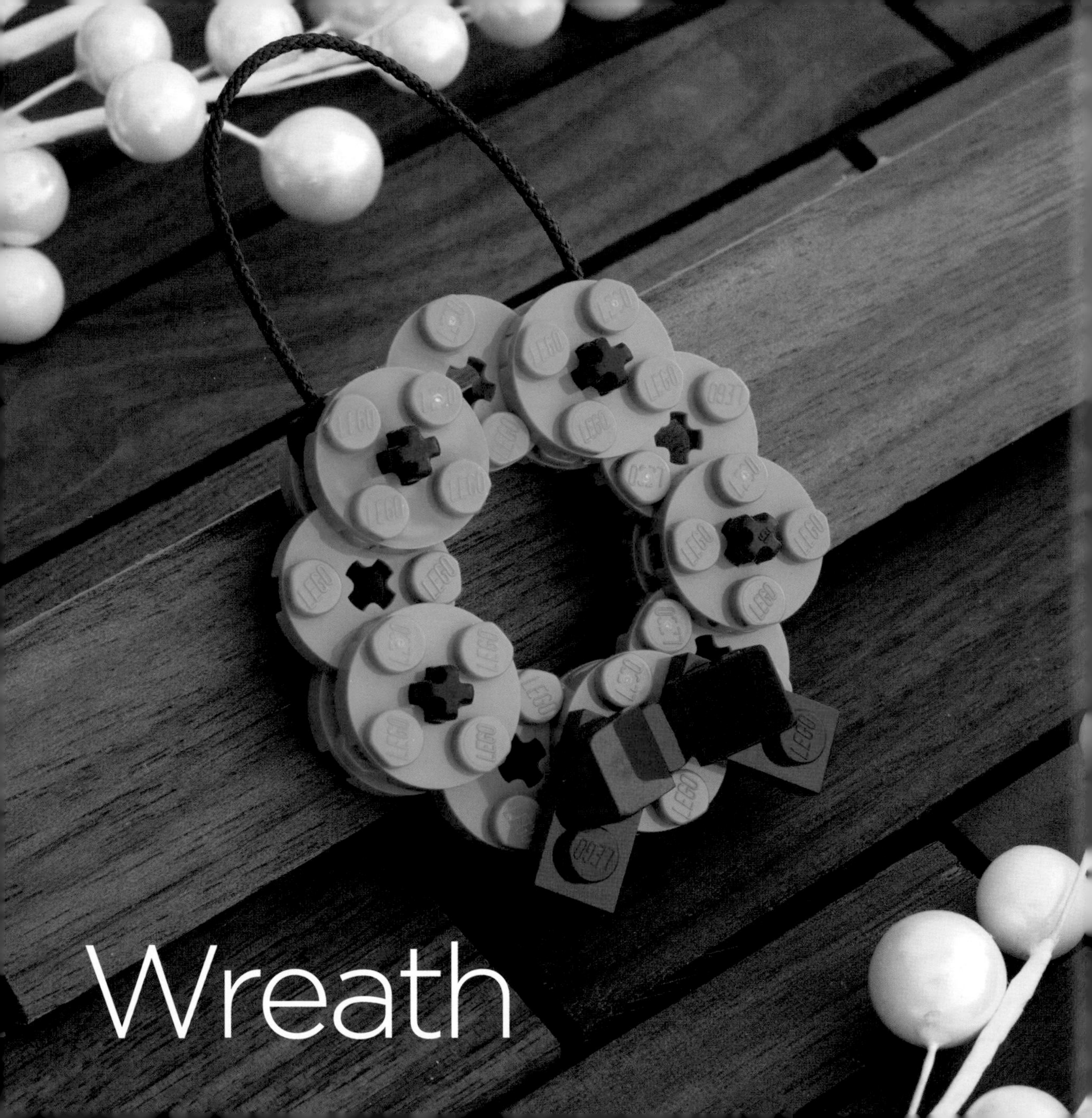

Wreath

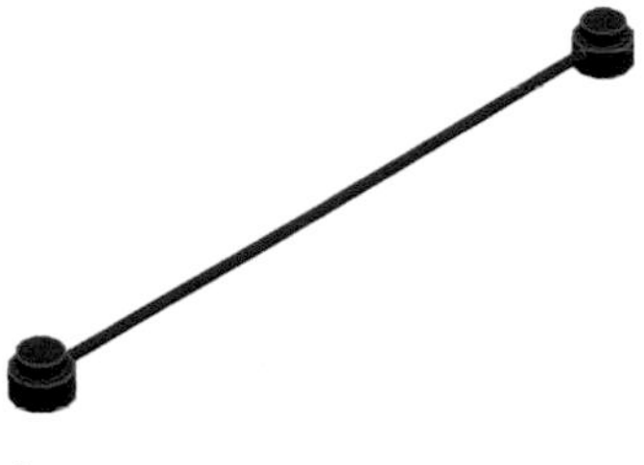

1x
6037558

4x
4142865

1x
74230

2x
4504379

15x
403228

1

2

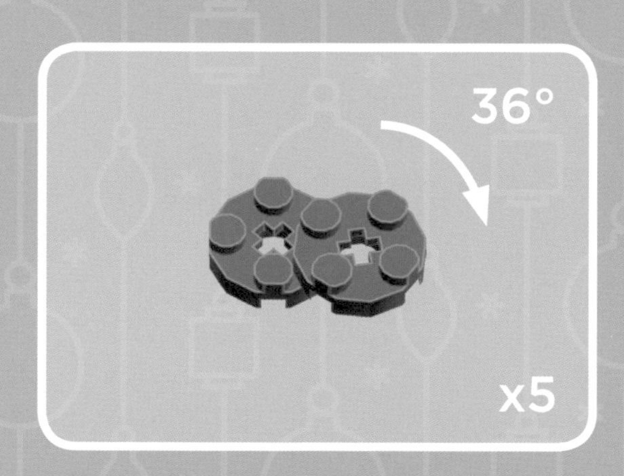

3

4

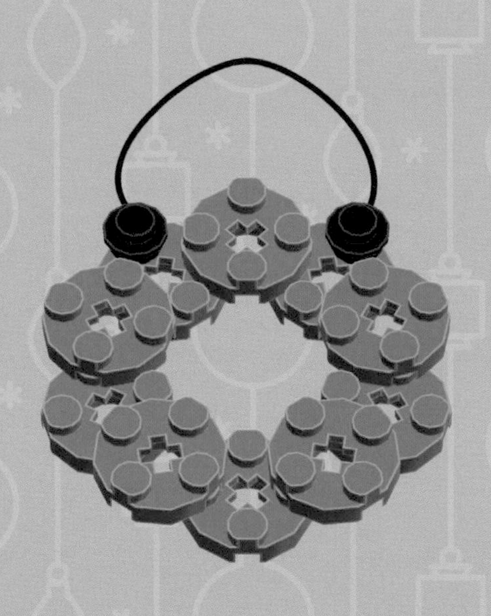

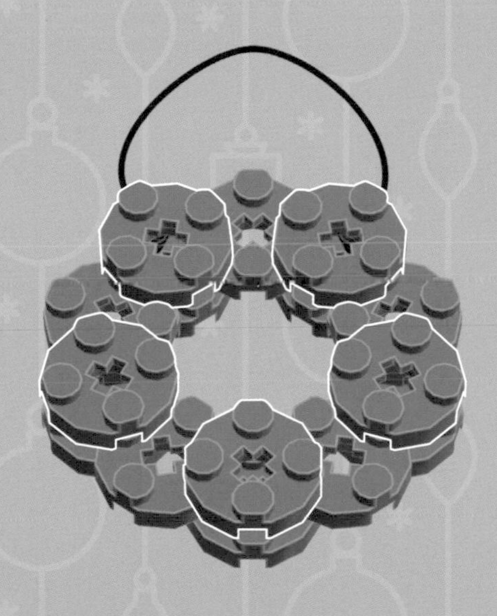

6

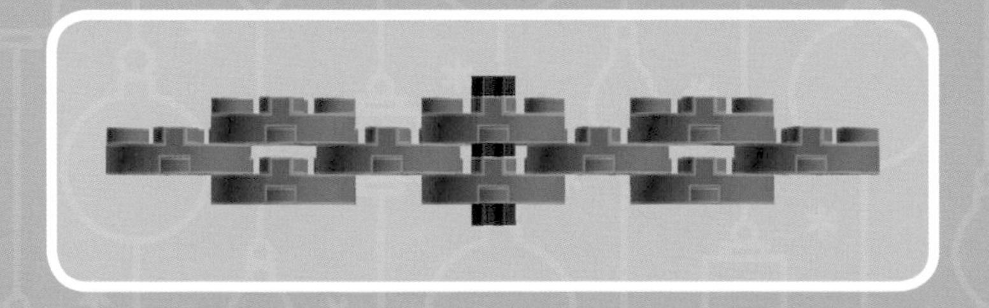

7

8

Present

1x
6010831

8x
6075074

4x
307021

8x
307001

4x
614101

4x
306821

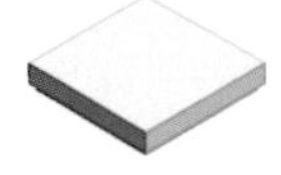

1x
306801

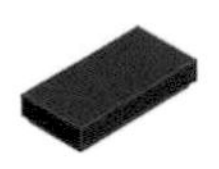

8x
306921

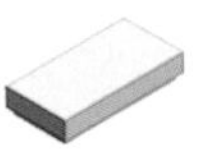

8x
306901

8x
302321

8x
4211502

2x
4211508

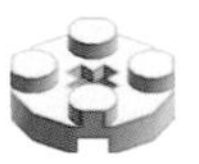

4x
403201

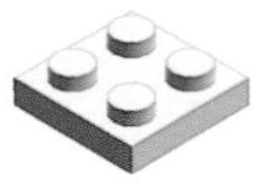

1x
302201

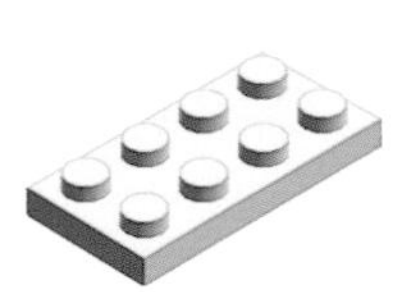

4x
302001

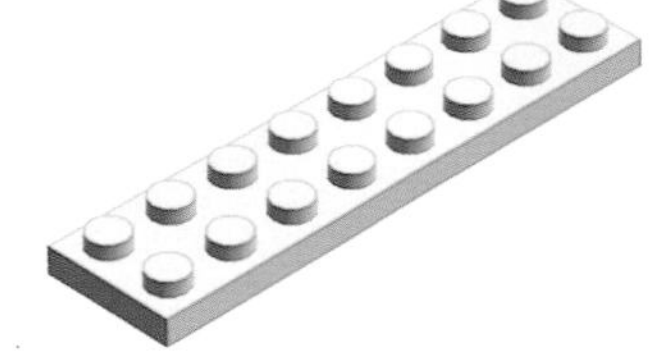

2x
303401

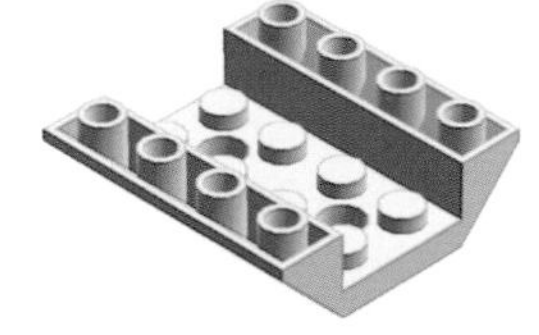

4x
4658973

1

2

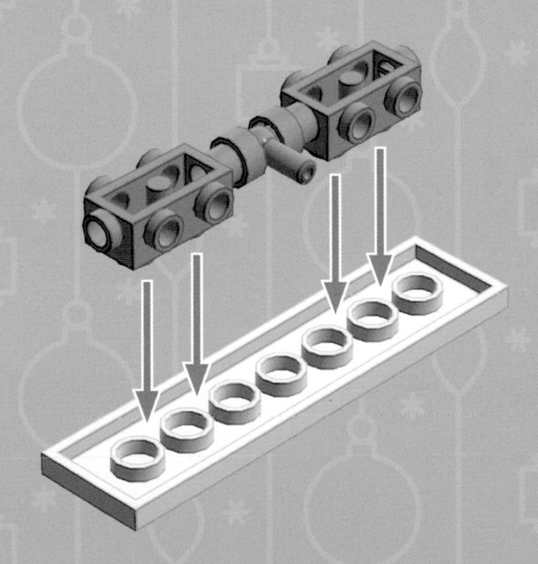

3

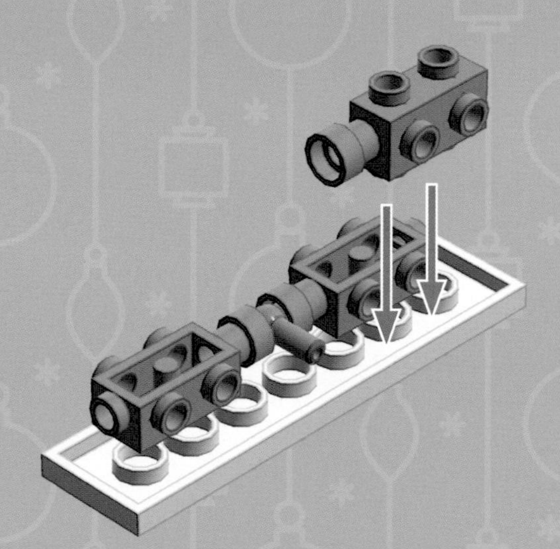

4

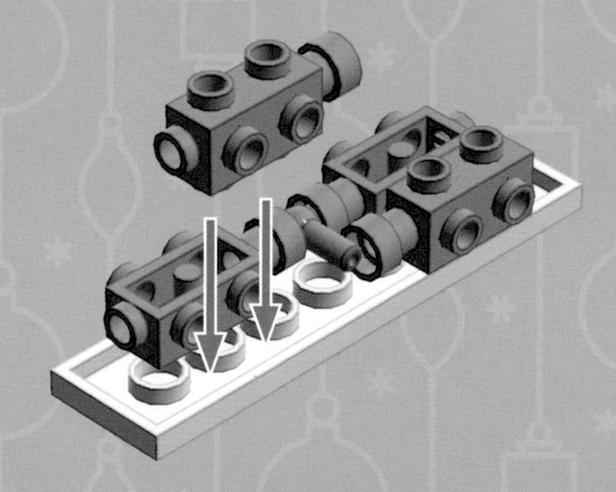

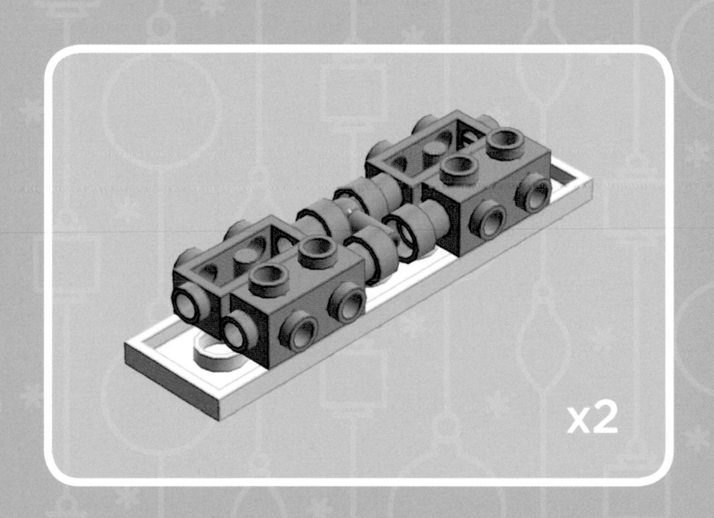
x2

5

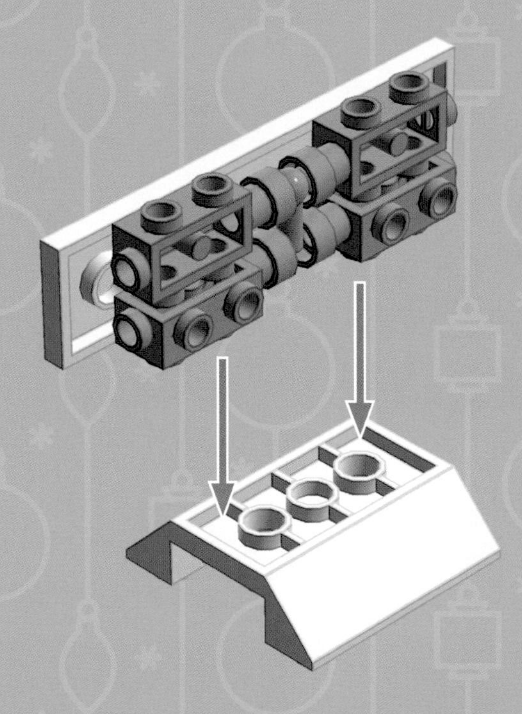

6

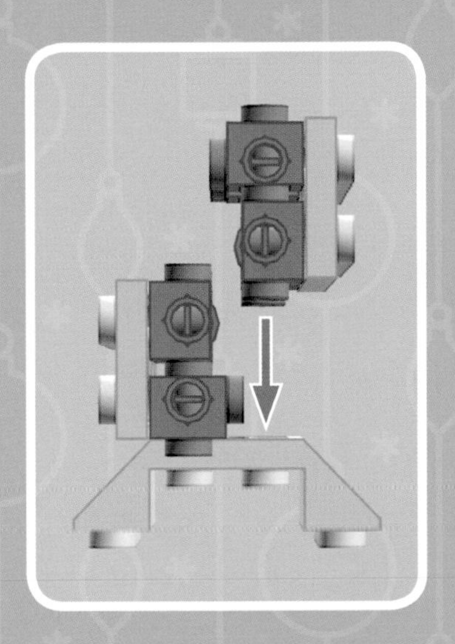

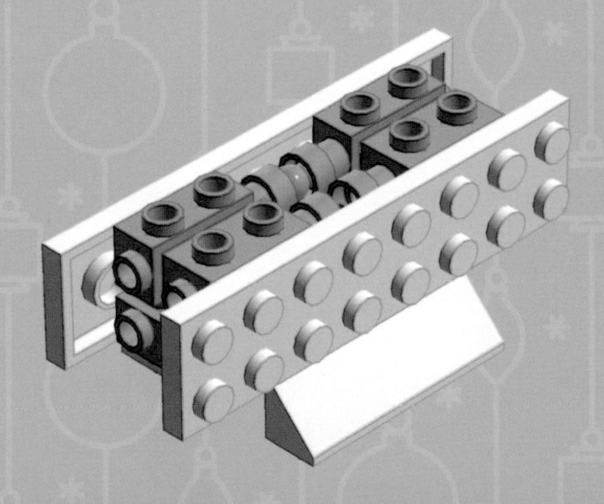

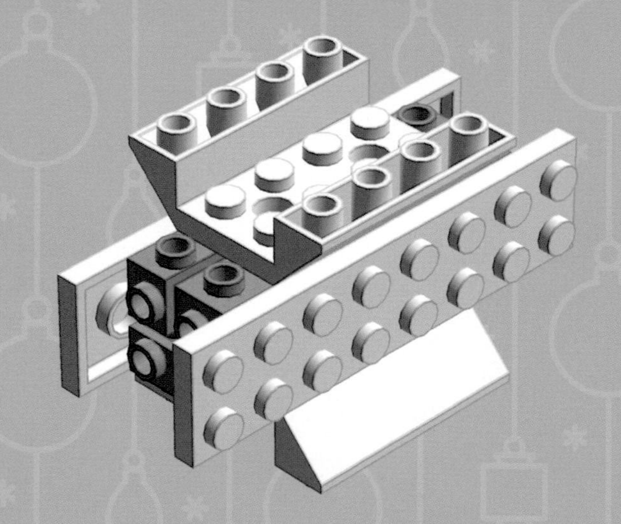

8

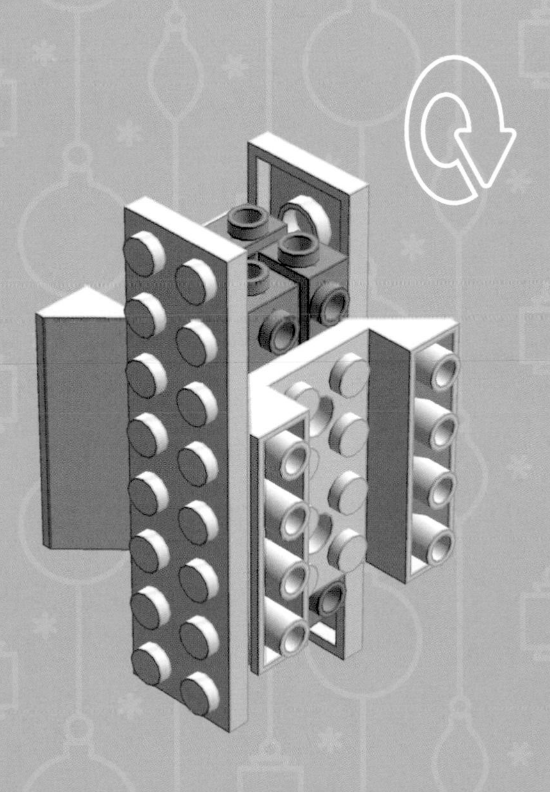

9

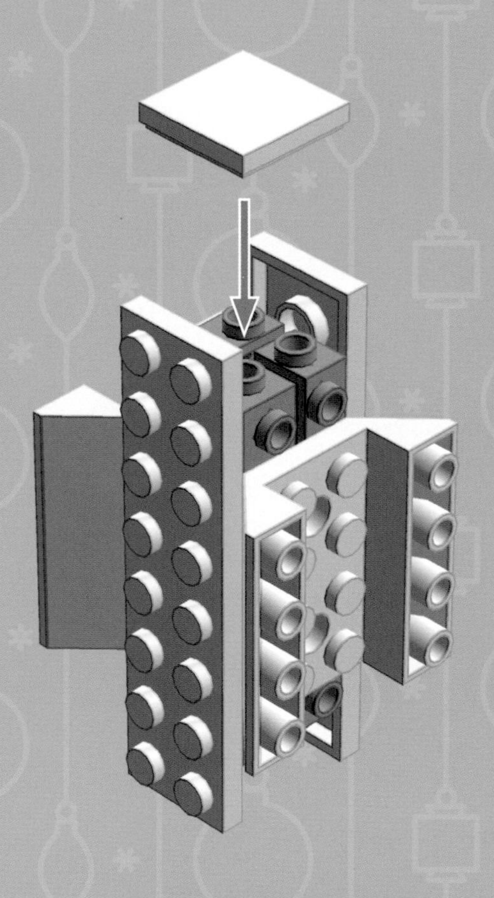

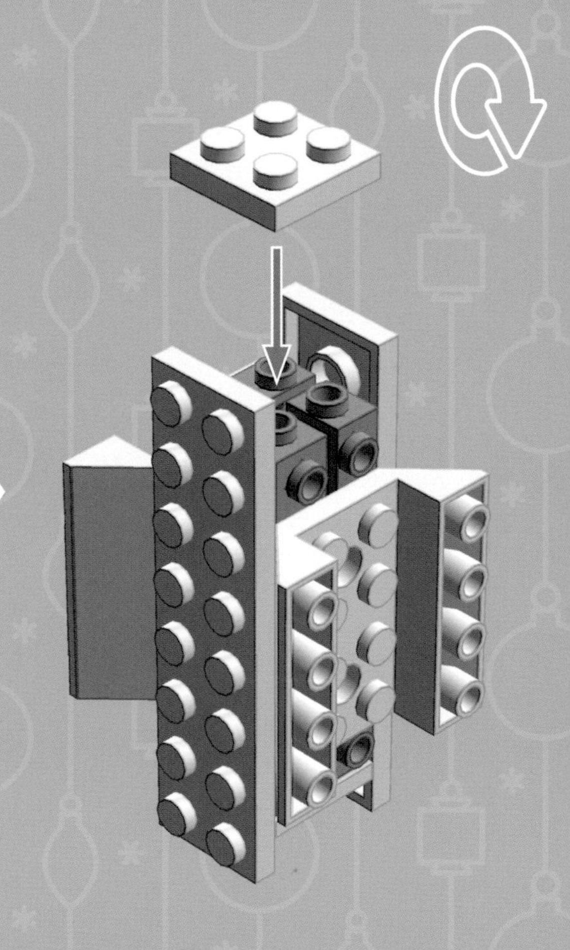

11

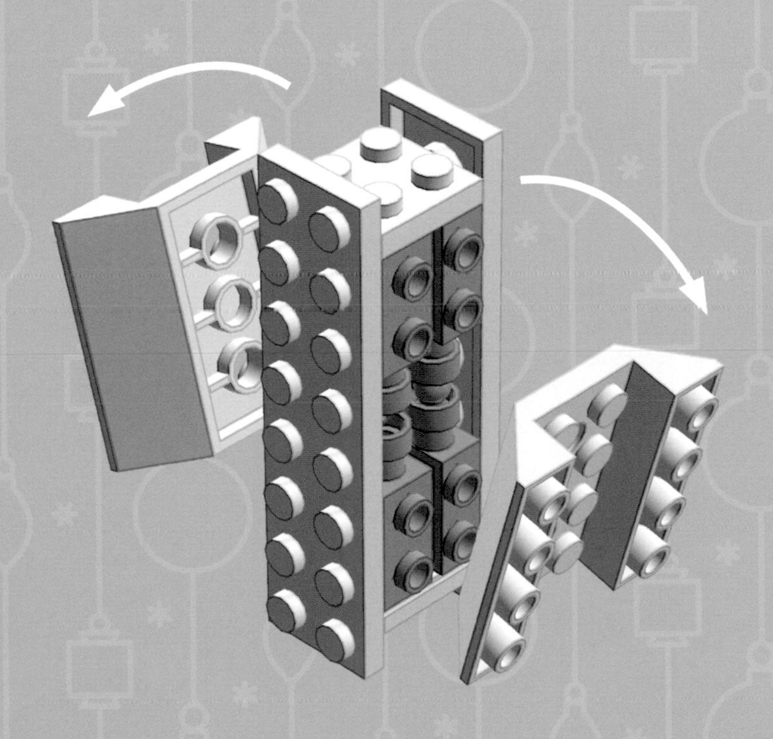

12

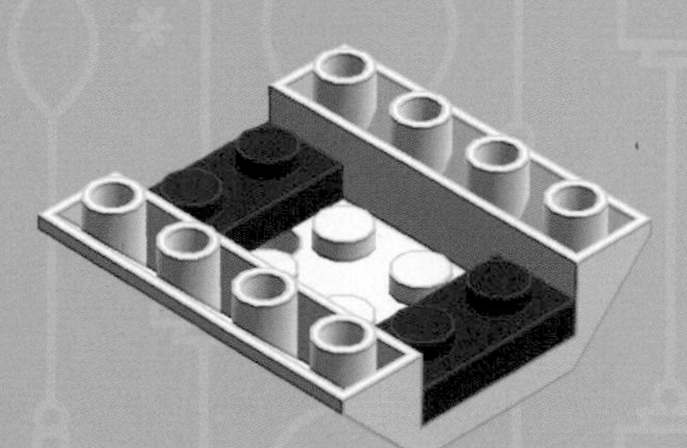

13

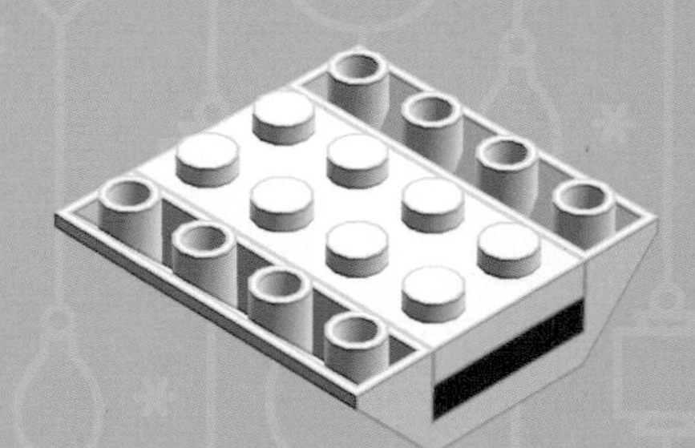

14

15

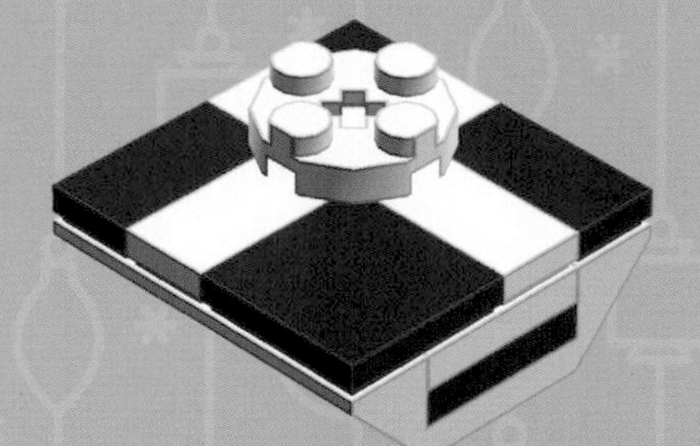

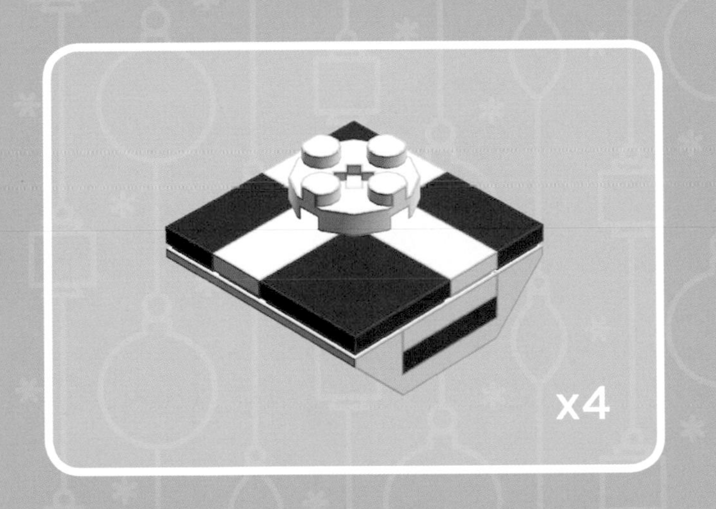
x4

16

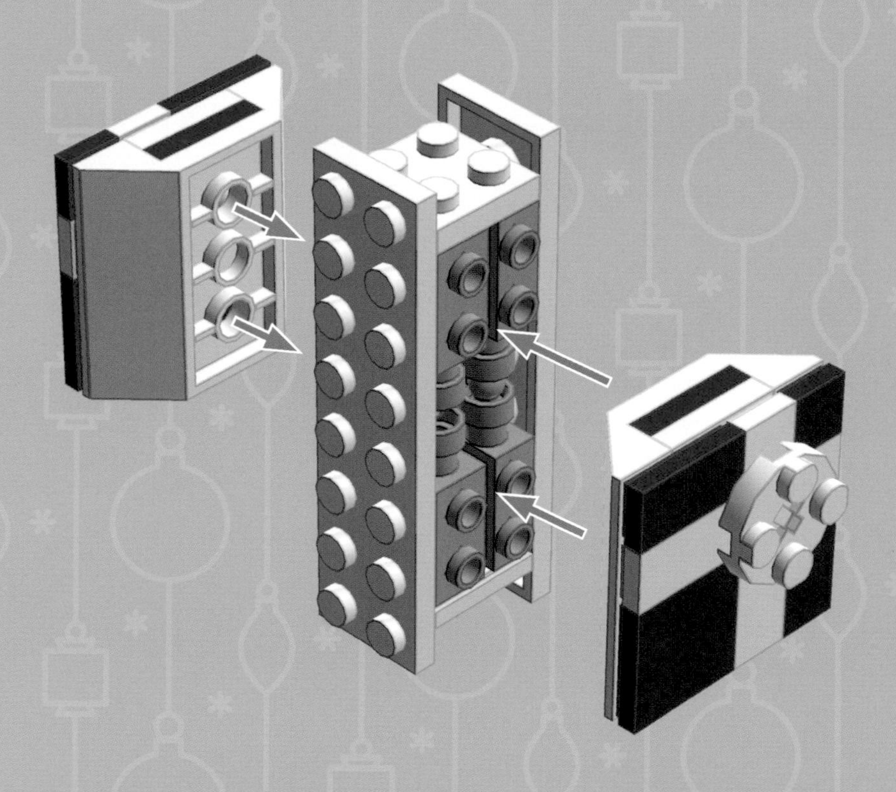

17

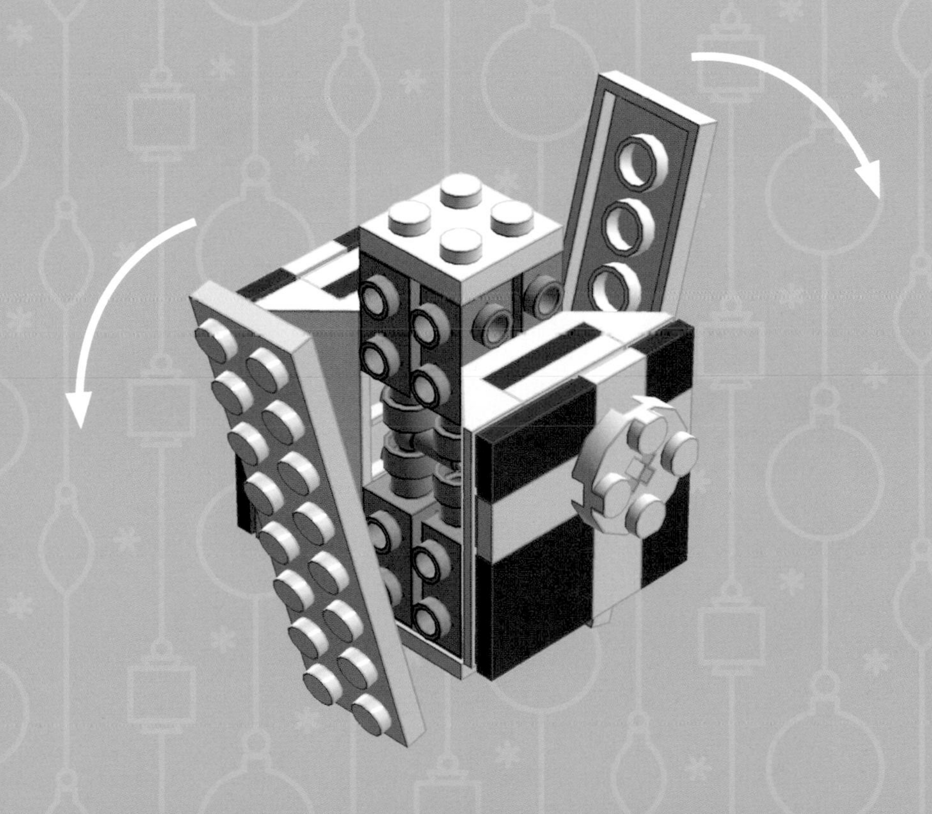

18

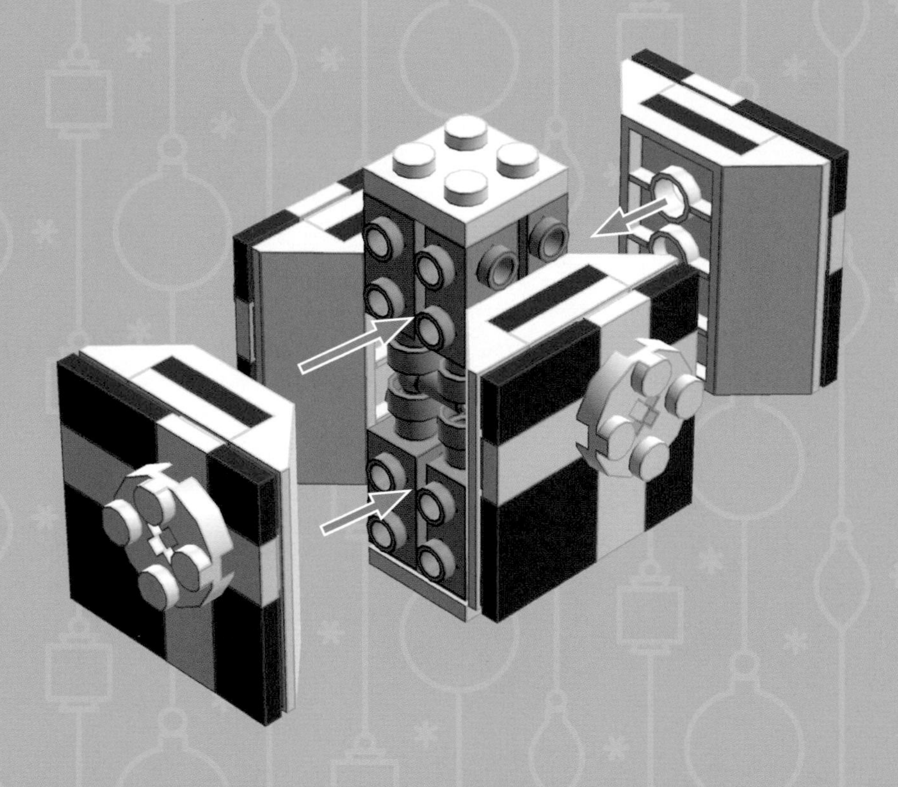

19

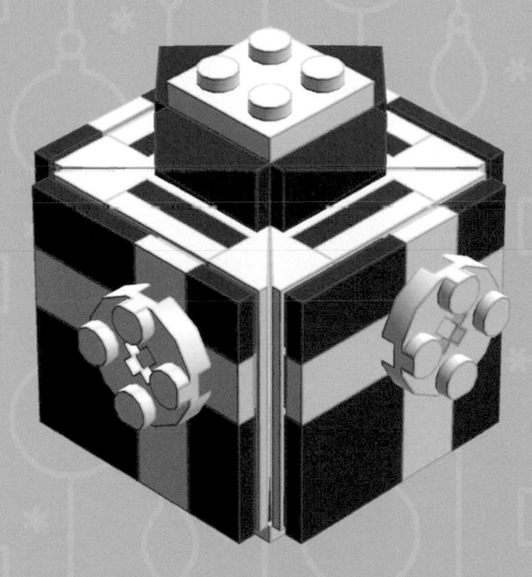

20

21

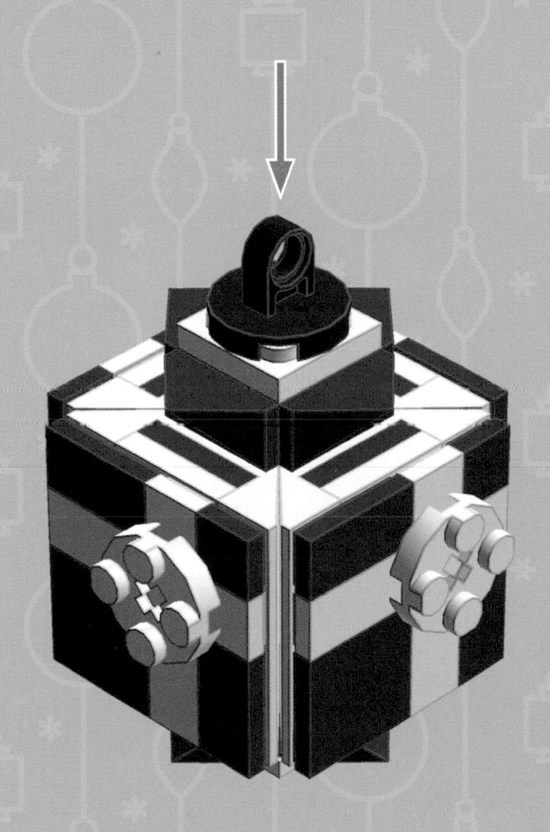

Christmas Tree

17x
4646844
4x
6100627
14x
614101
3x
302401
10x
302421
10x
6073040
1x
306228
4x
4211183
1x
6029774
1x
302201
2x
4581308
1x
4179580
4x
4211222
8x
4515368
4x
362326
4x
371028
4x
6039869
2x
6052369
4x
4621946
8x
4543262
12x
4621947
8x
4543259
1x
4614226
2x
6017001

1

3

5
x2

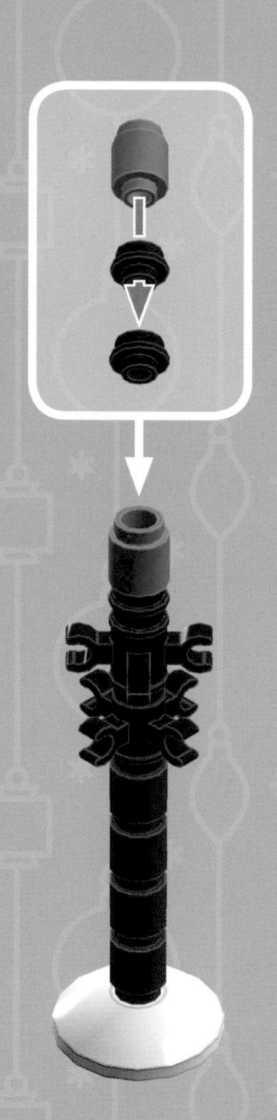
6

7

8

9

10

11

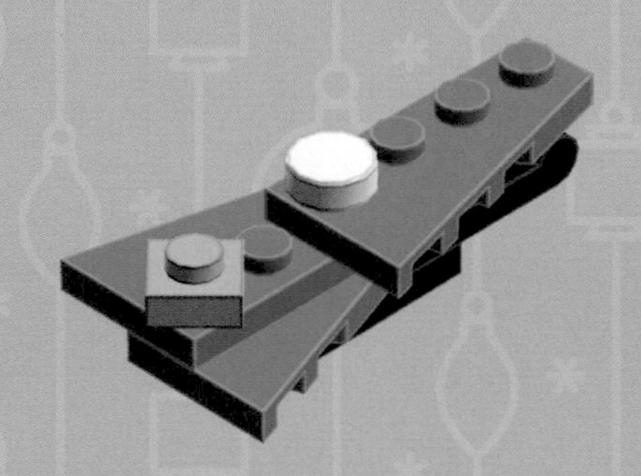

12

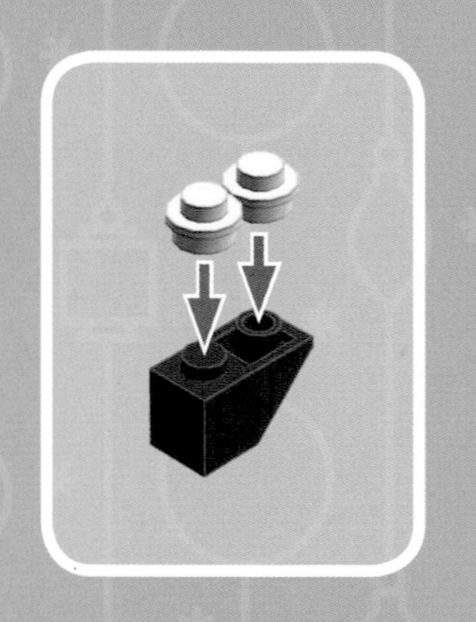

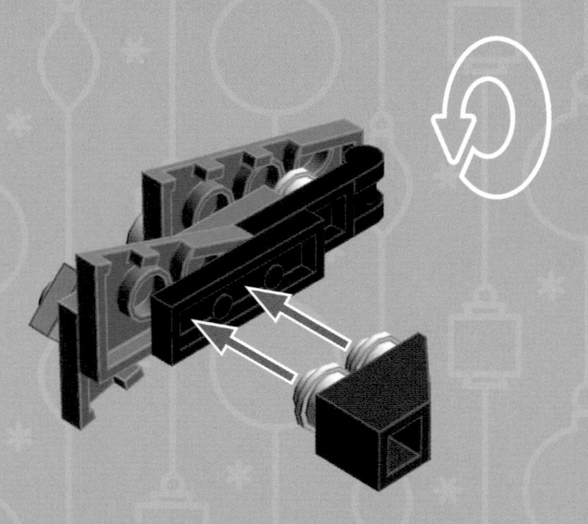

13

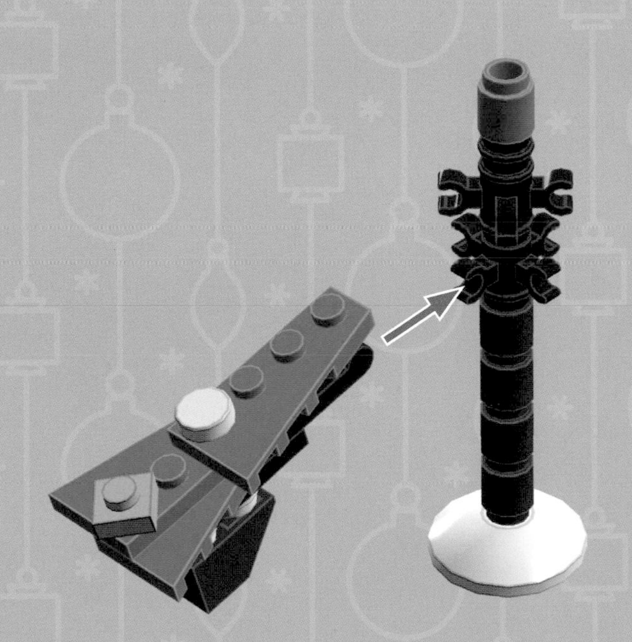

14

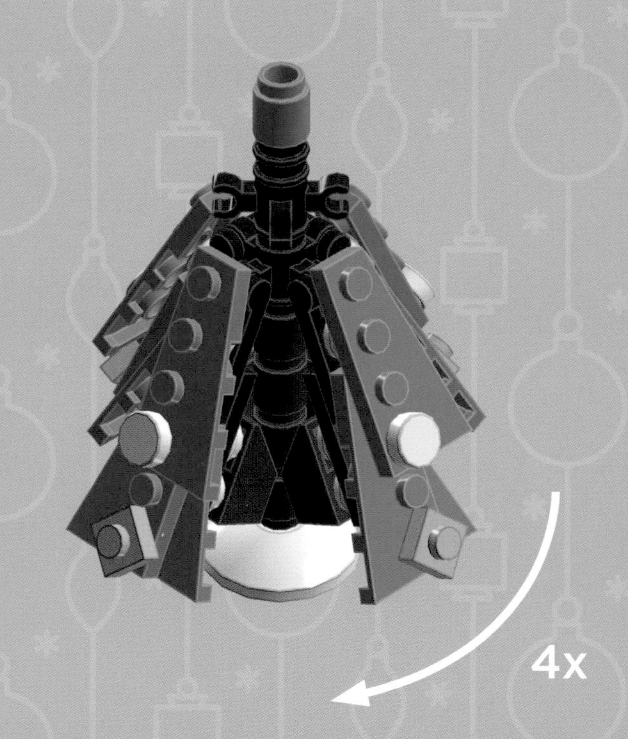

15

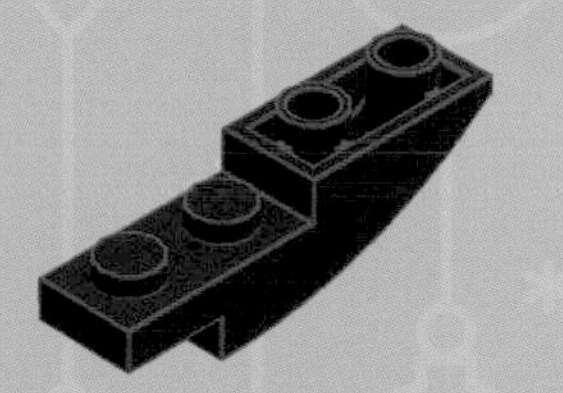

16

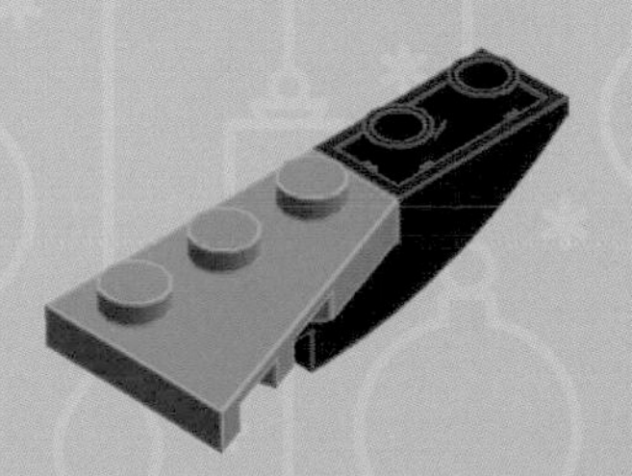

17

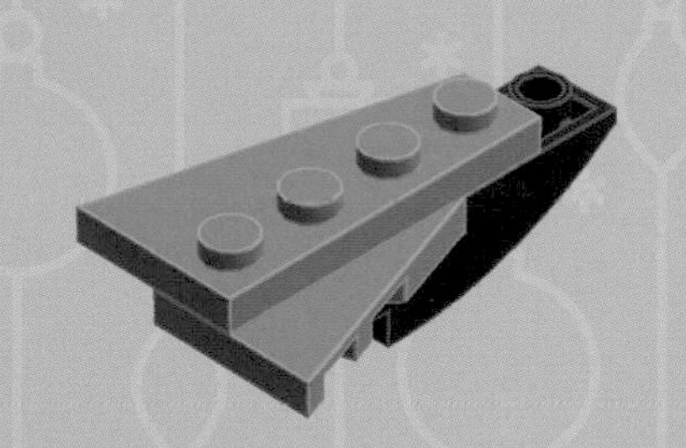

18

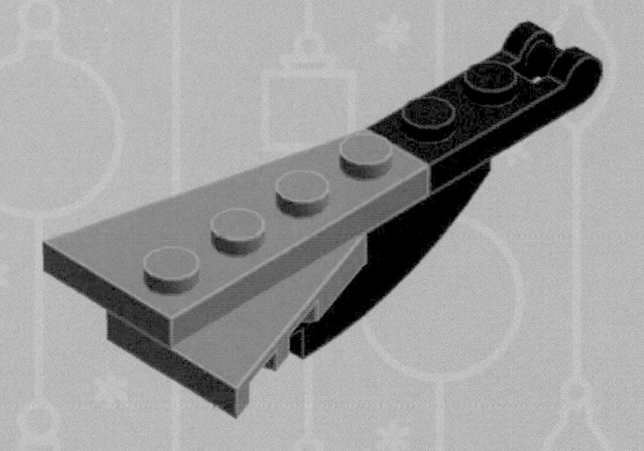

19

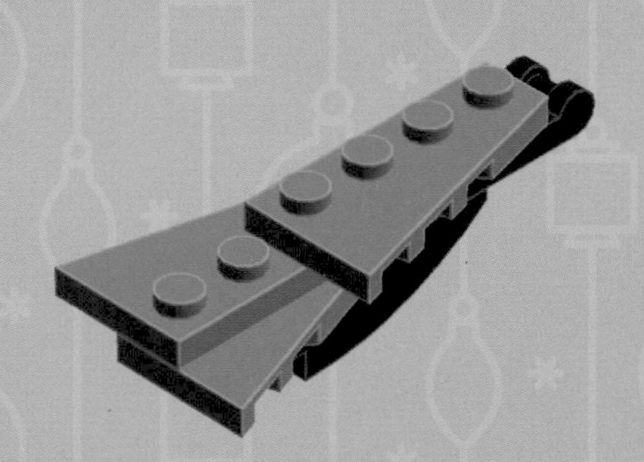

20

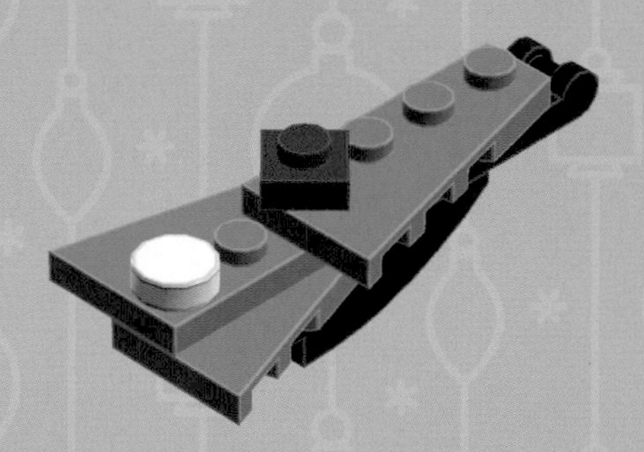

21

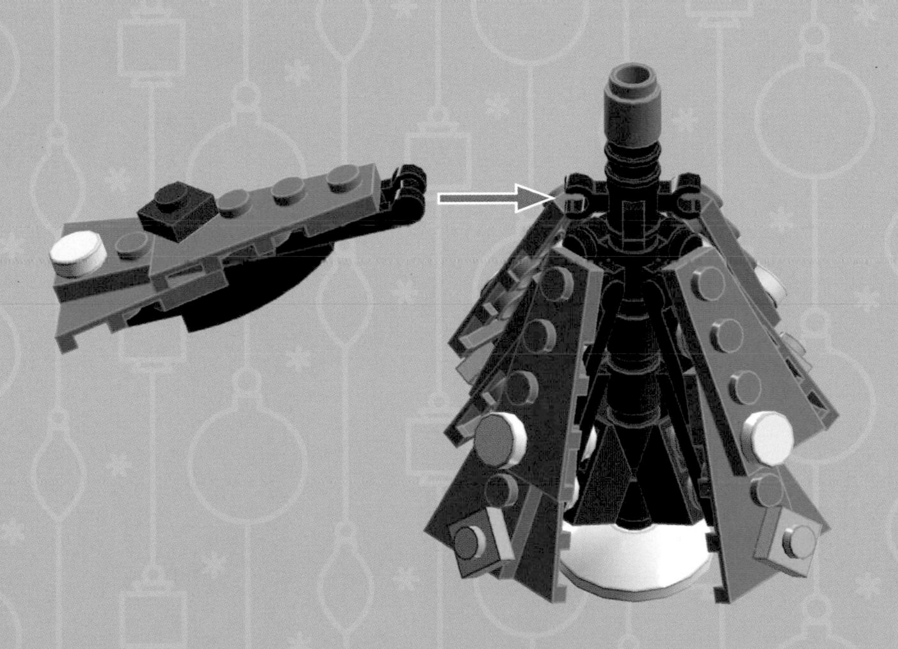

22

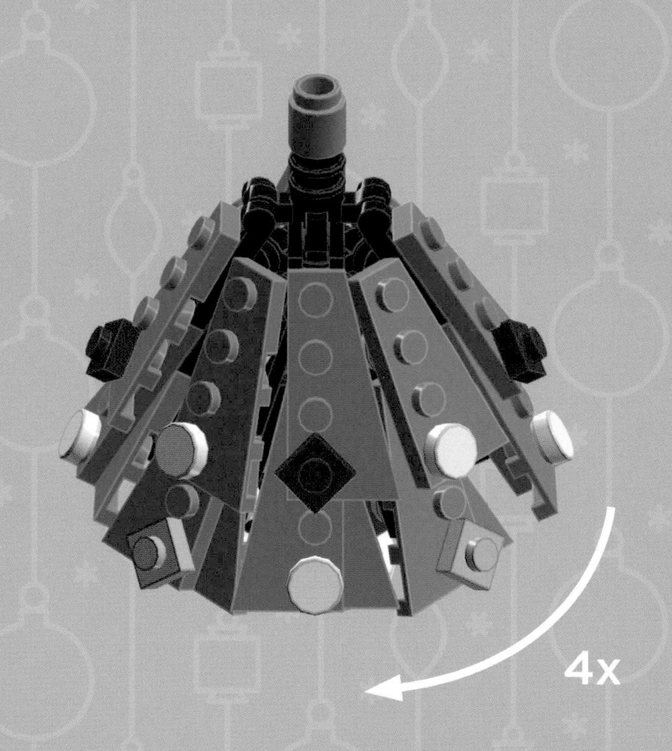

23

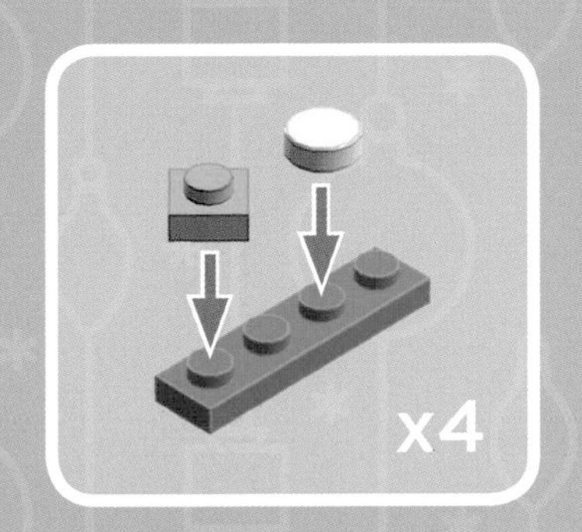

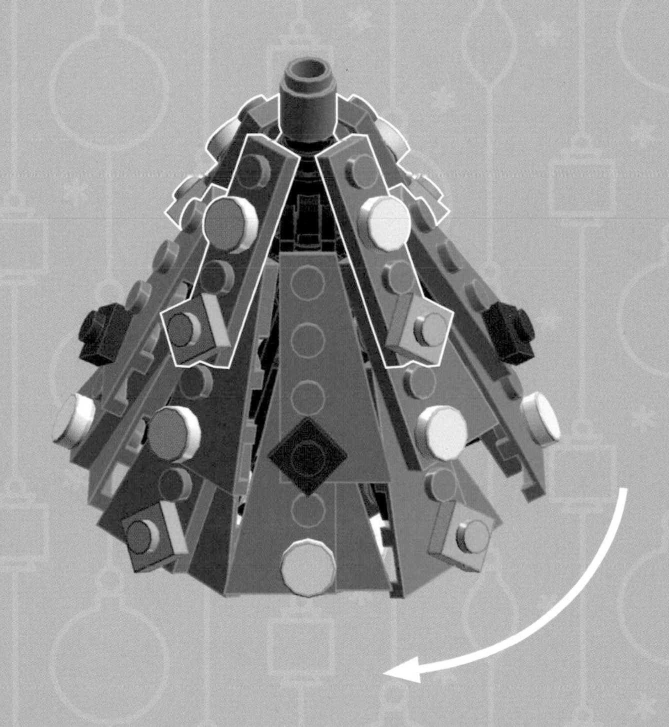

24

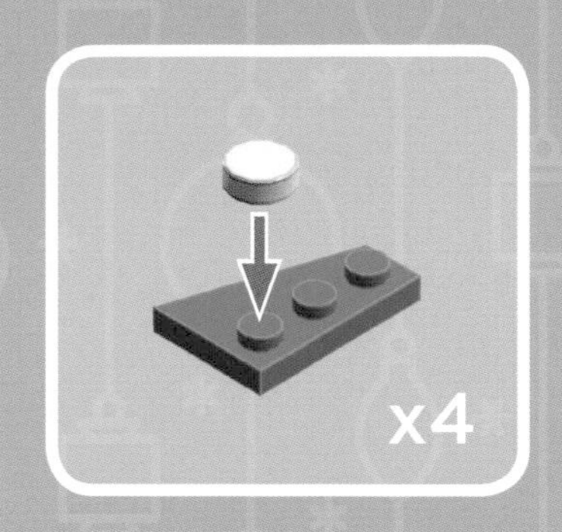

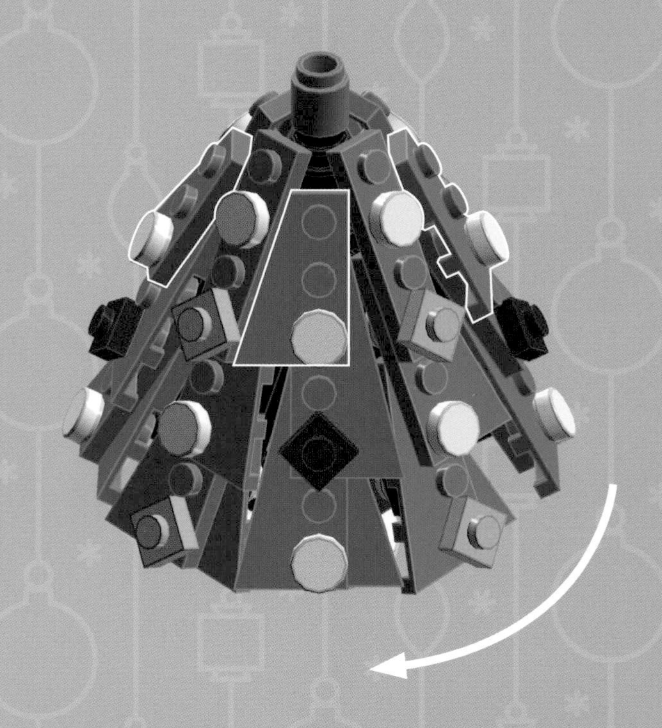

25

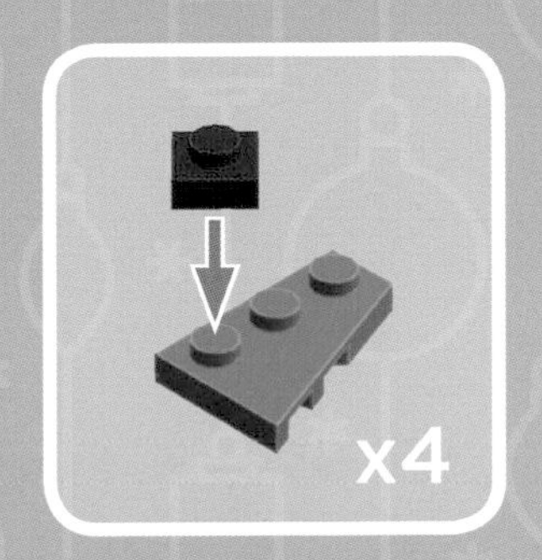

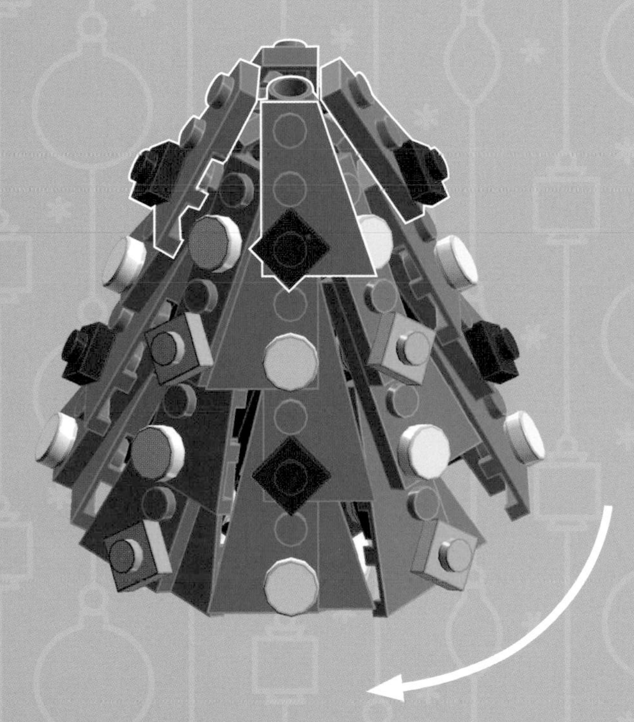

26

27

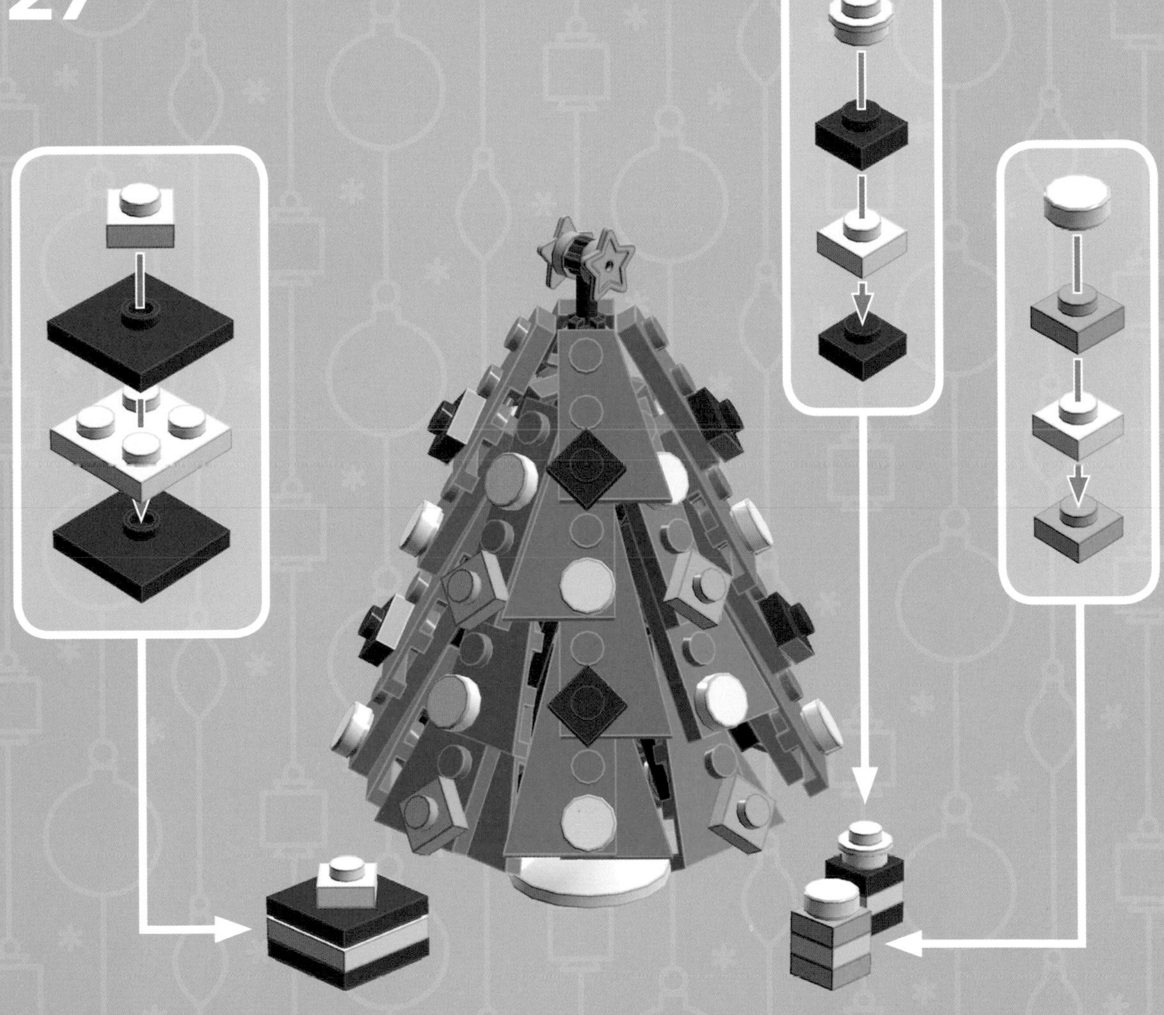

Gingerbread House

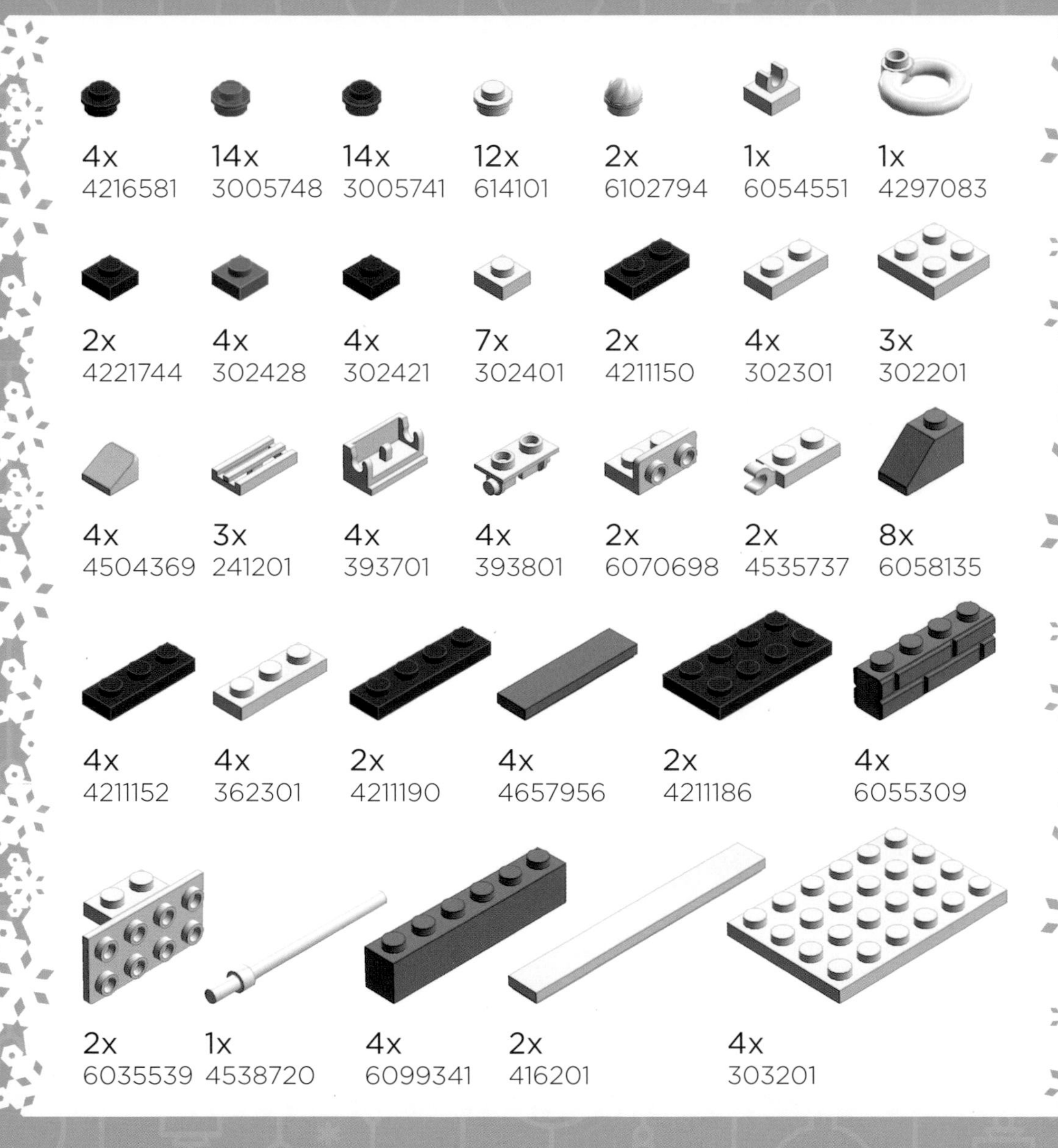
4x 4216581
14x 3005748
14x 3005741
12x 614101
2x 6102794
1x 6054551
1x 4297083
2x 4221744
4x 302428
4x 302421
7x 302401
2x 4211150
4x 302301
3x 302201
4x 4504369
3x 241201
4x 393701
4x 393801
2x 6070698
2x 4535737
8x 6058135
4x 4211152
4x 362301
2x 4211190
4x 4657956
2x 4211186
4x 6055309
2x 6035539
1x 4538720
4x 6099341
2x 416201
4x 303201

1

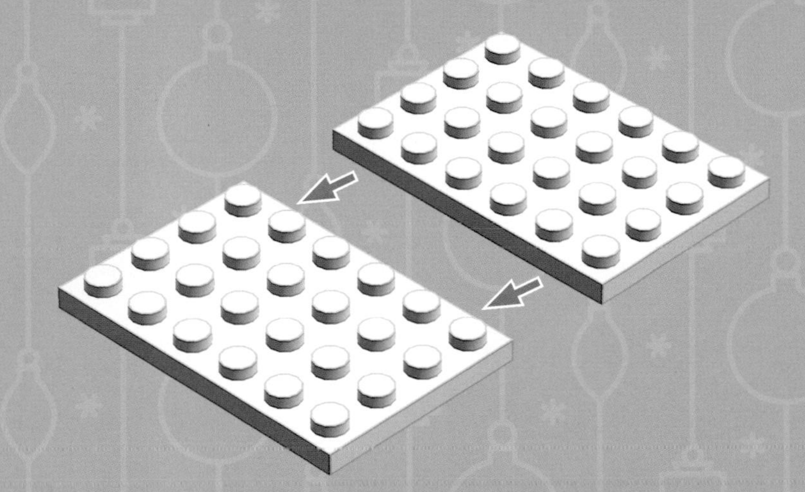

2

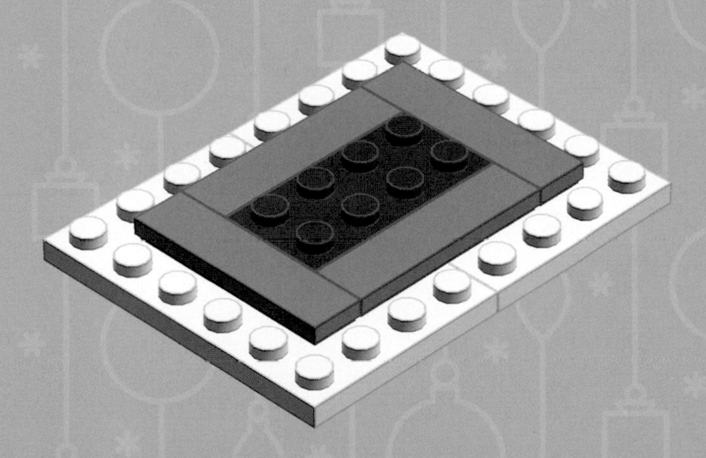

3

4

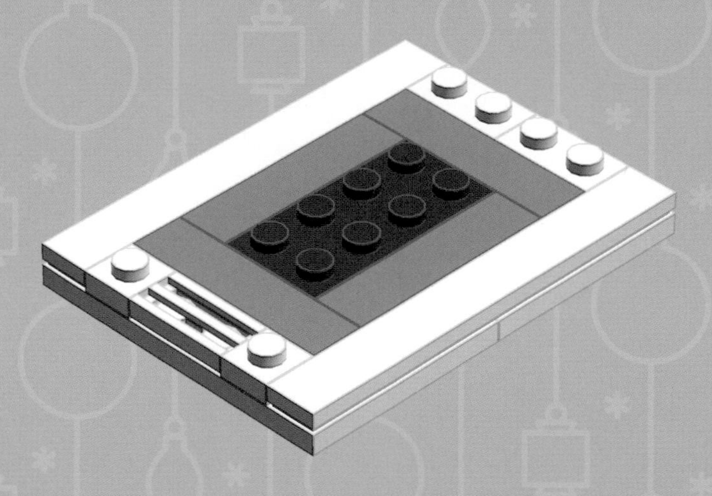

5

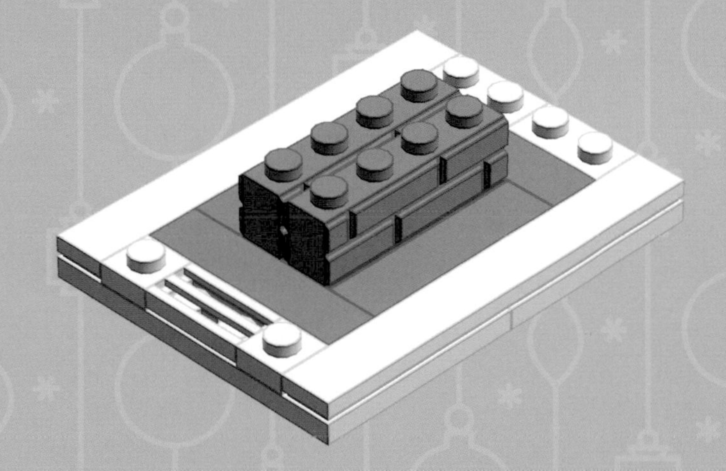

6

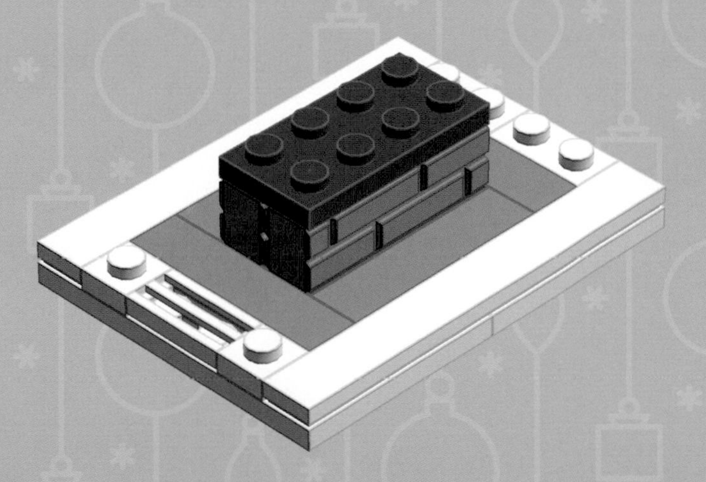

7

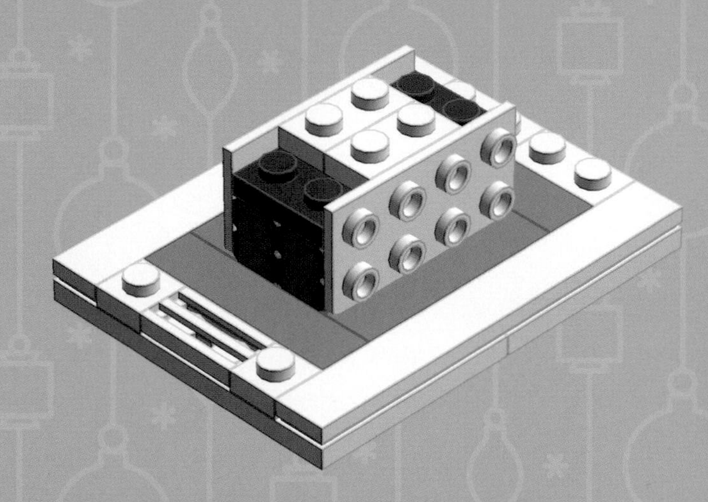

8

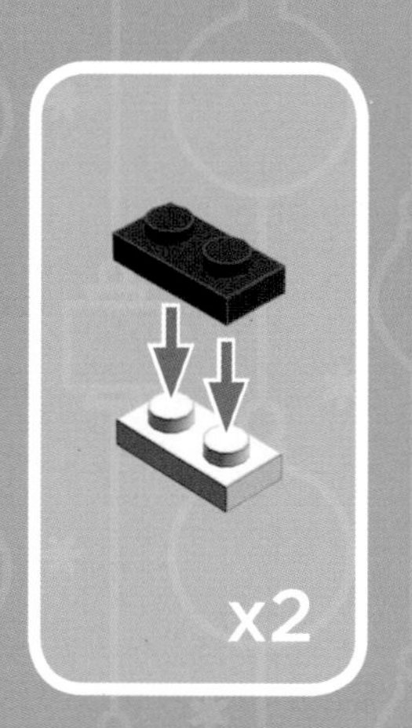

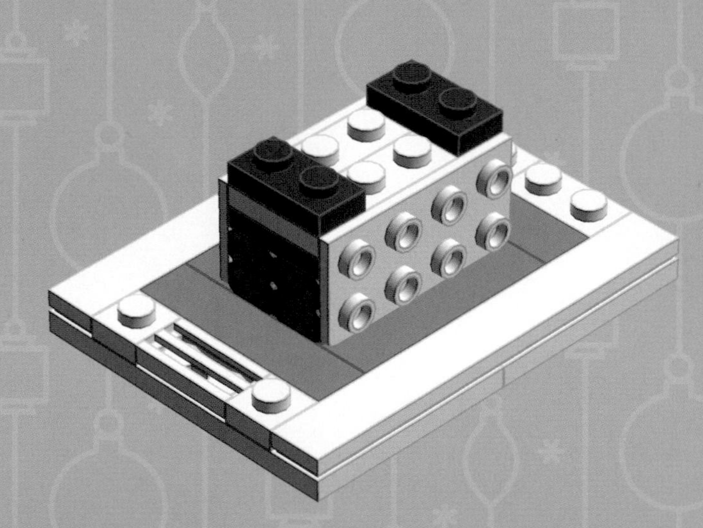

9

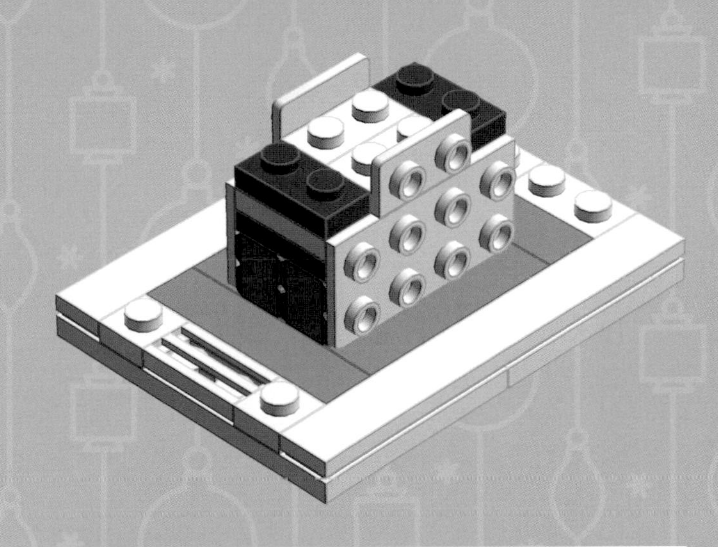

10

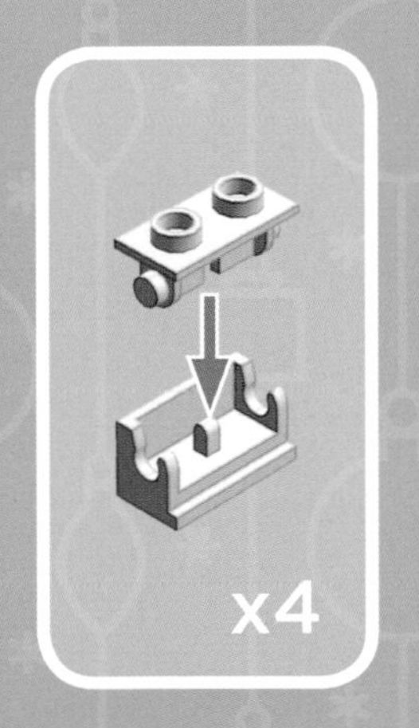

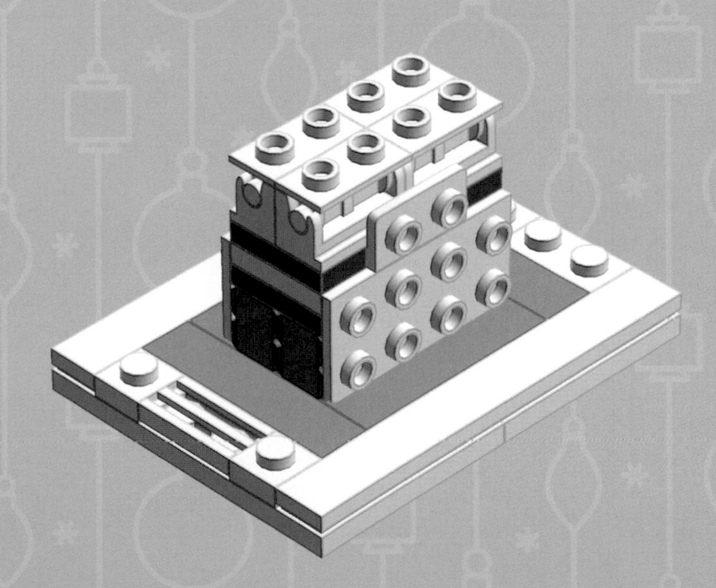

11

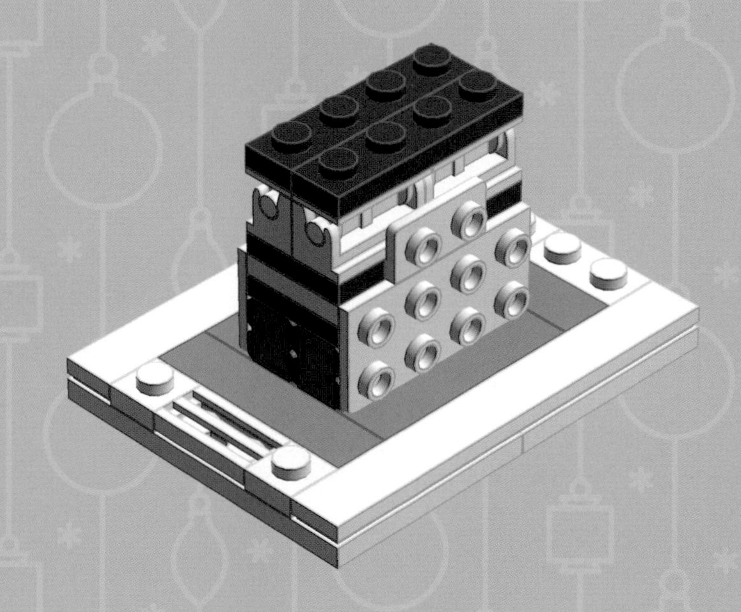

12

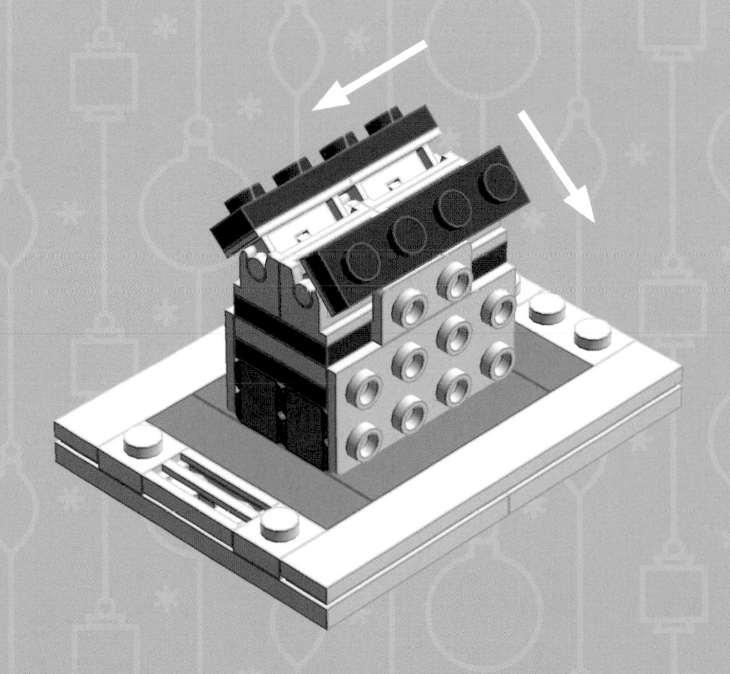

13

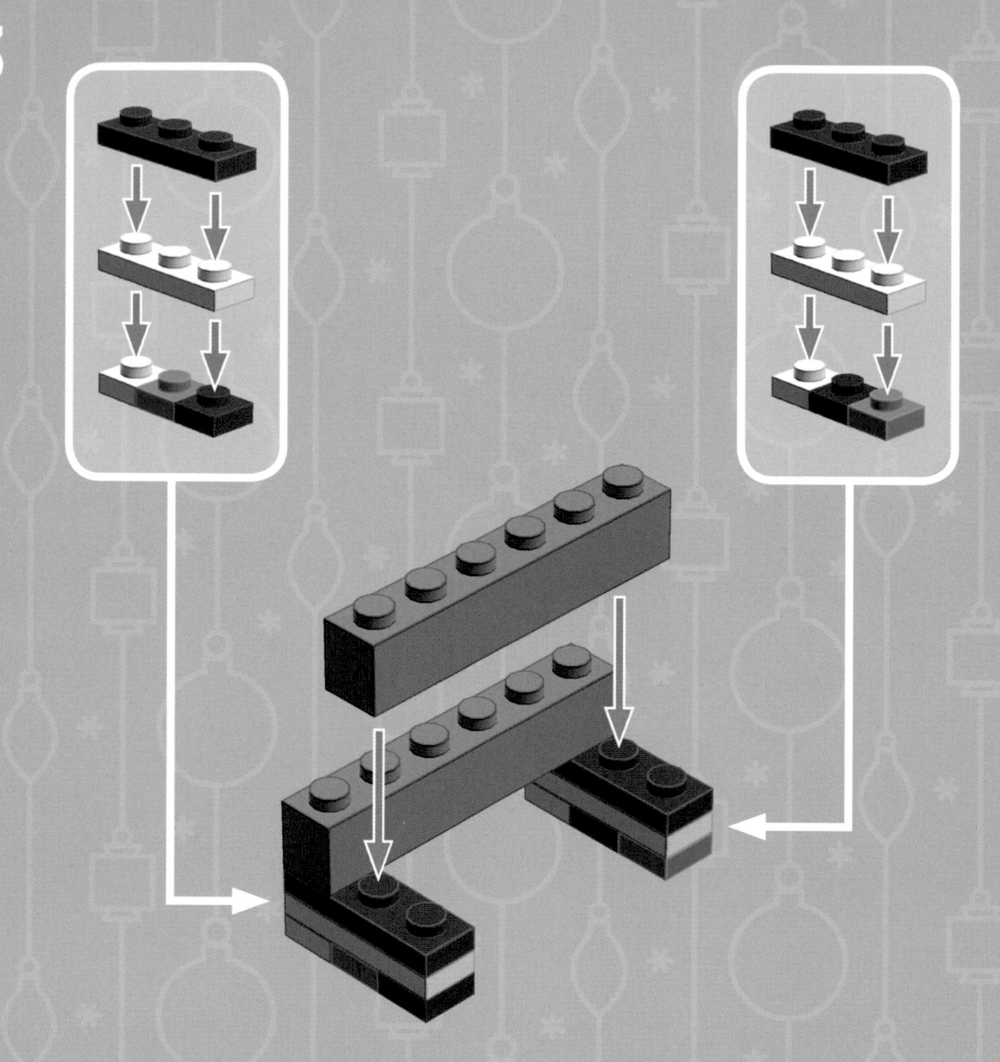

14

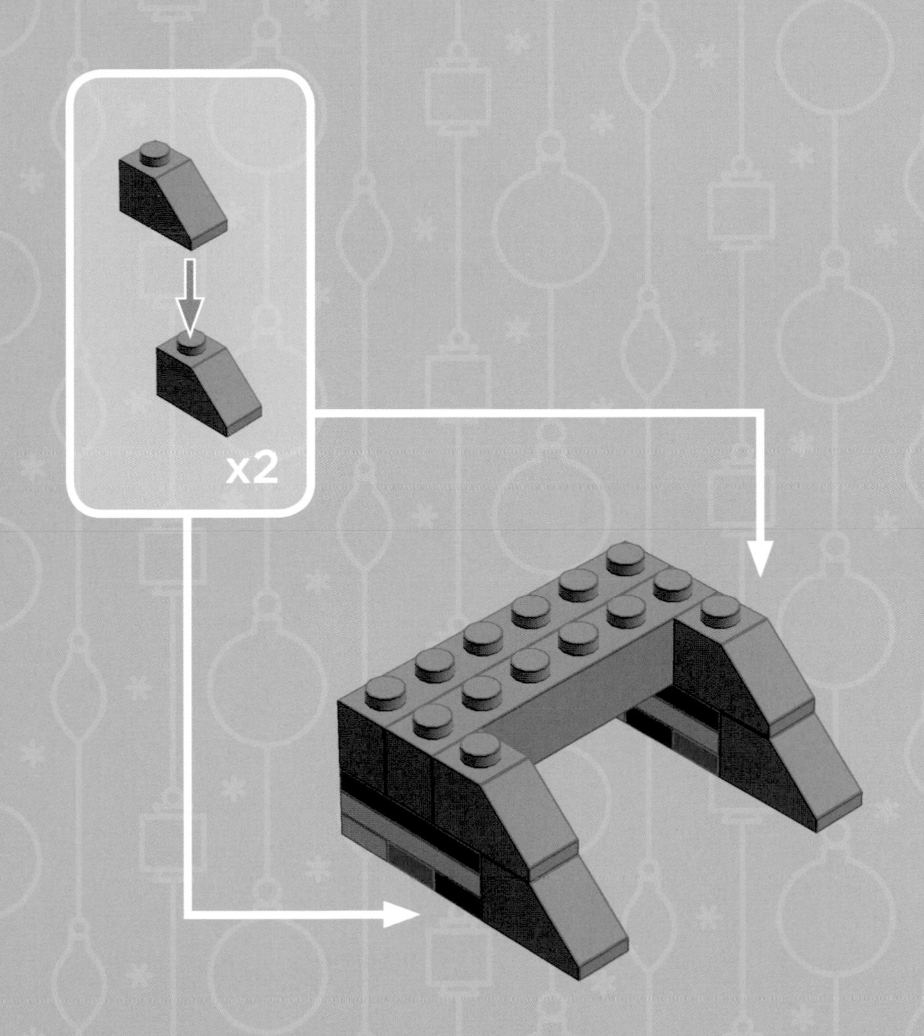

15

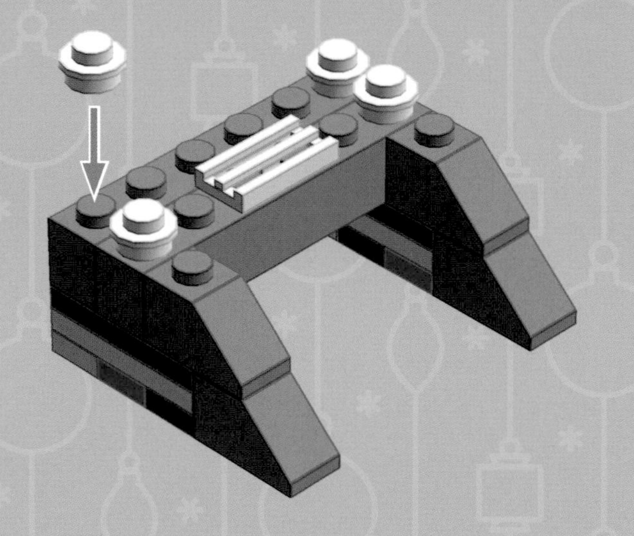

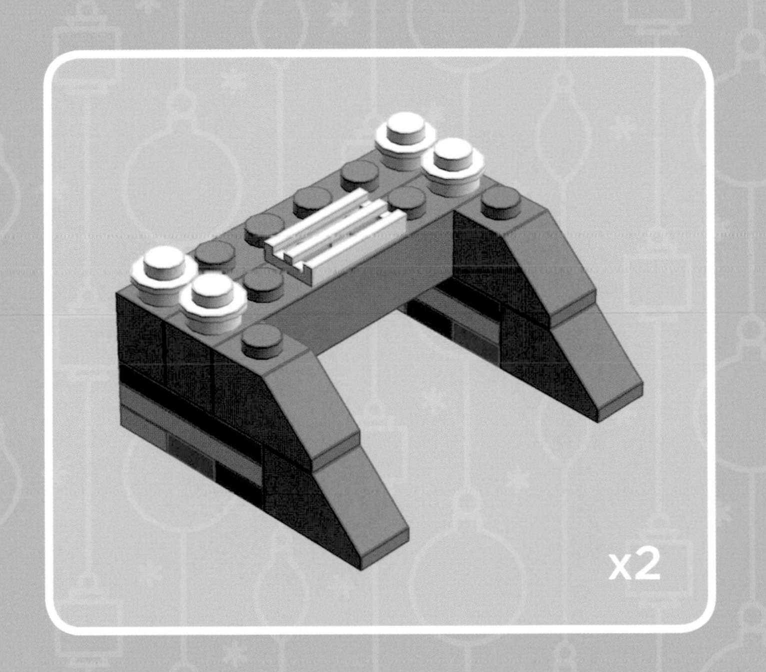
x2

16

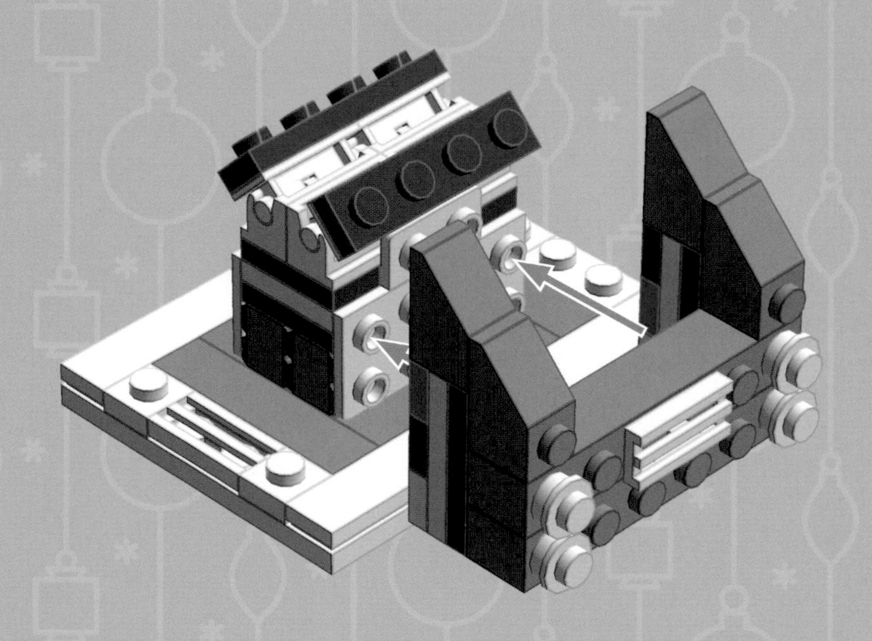

17

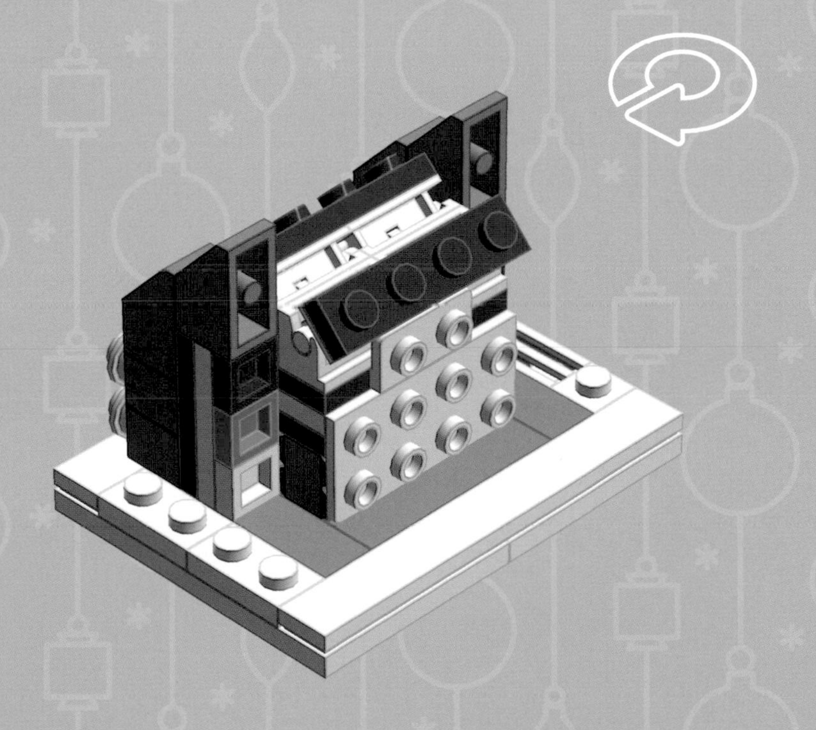

18

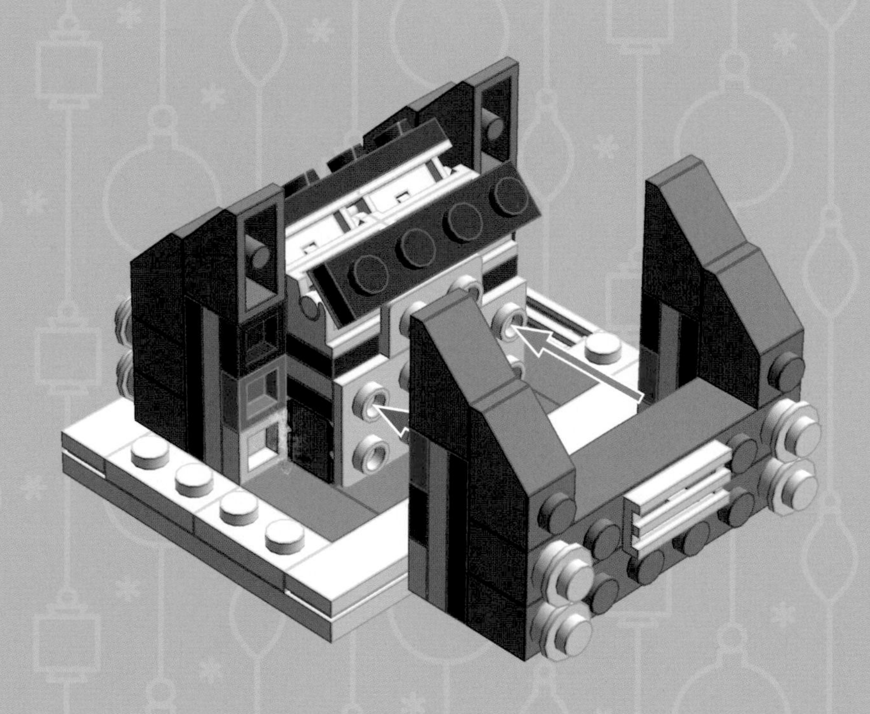

19

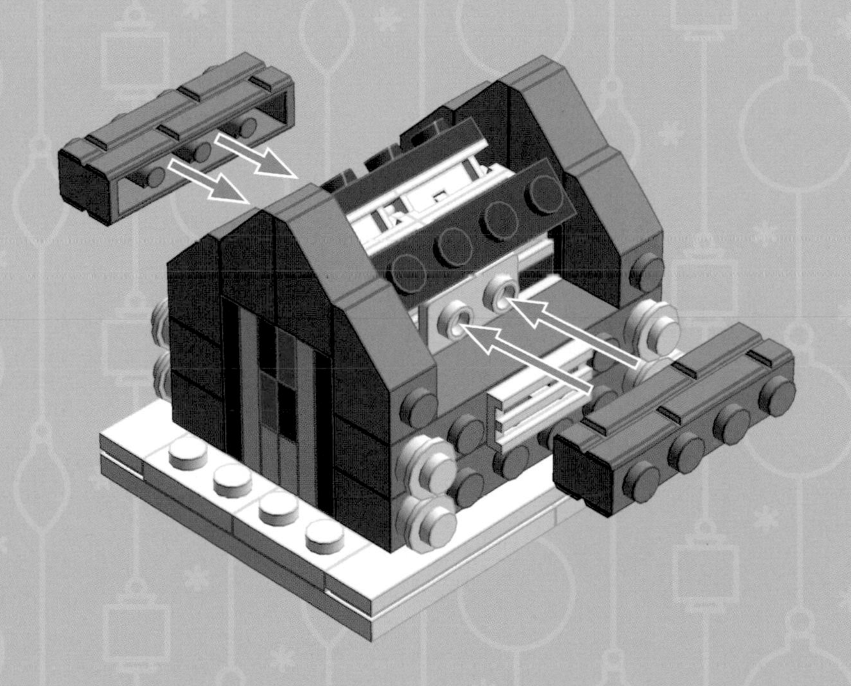

20

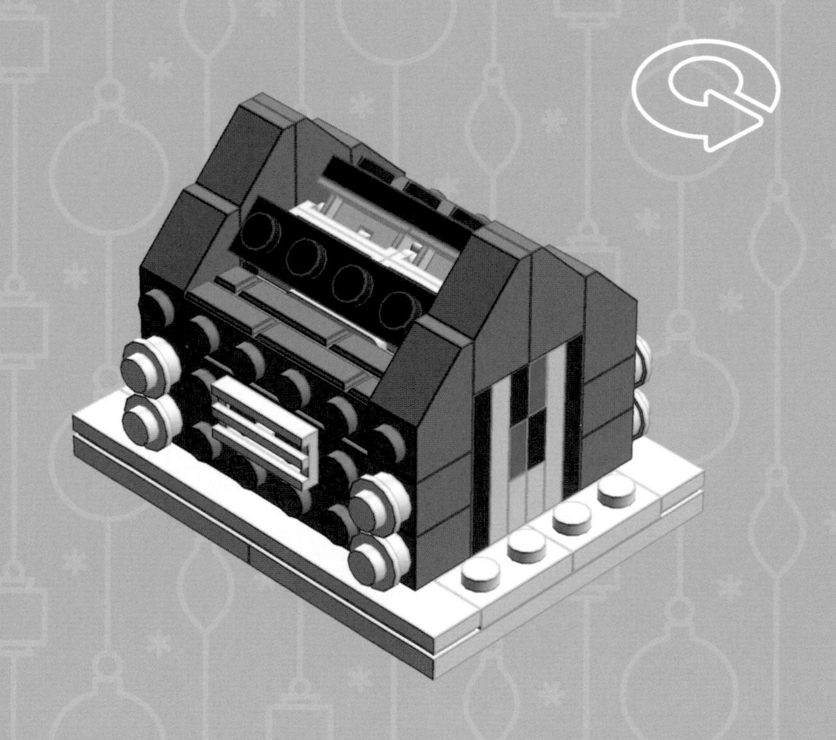

21

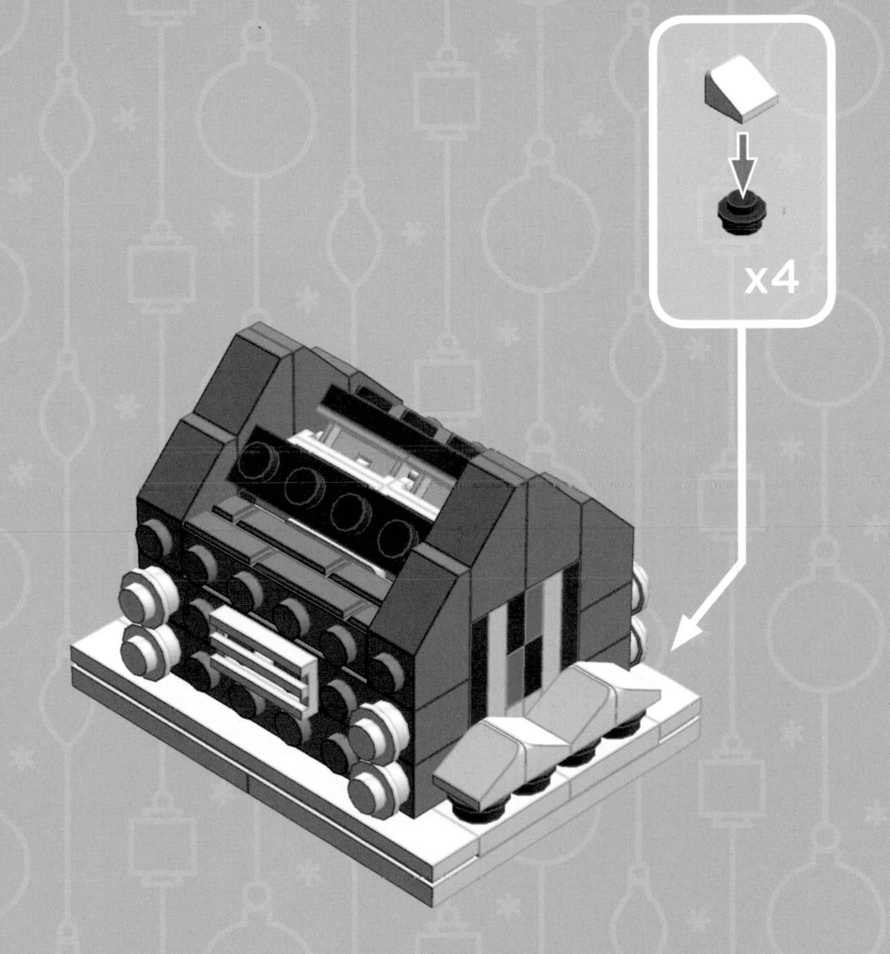

22

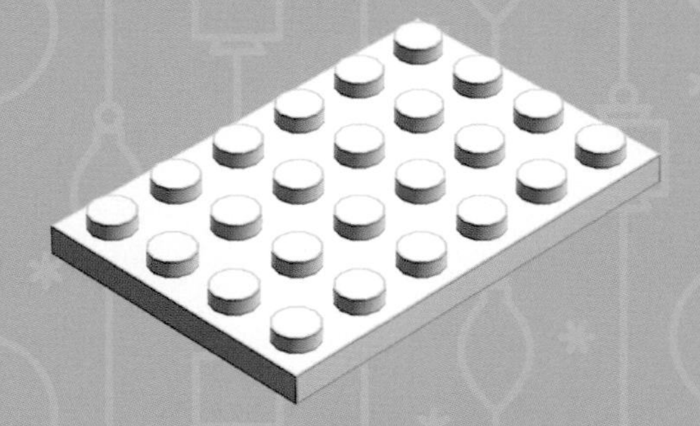

23

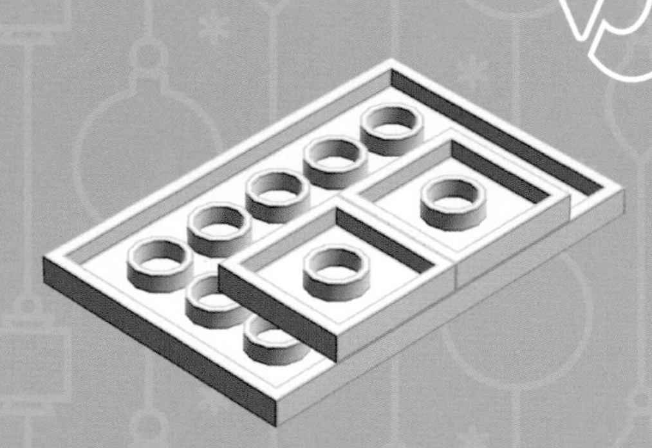

24

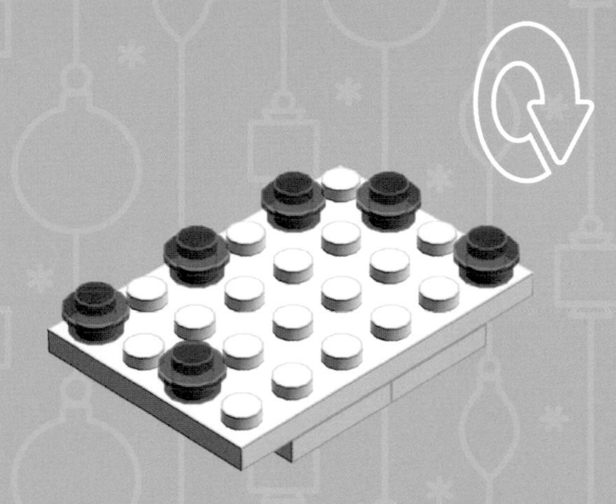

25

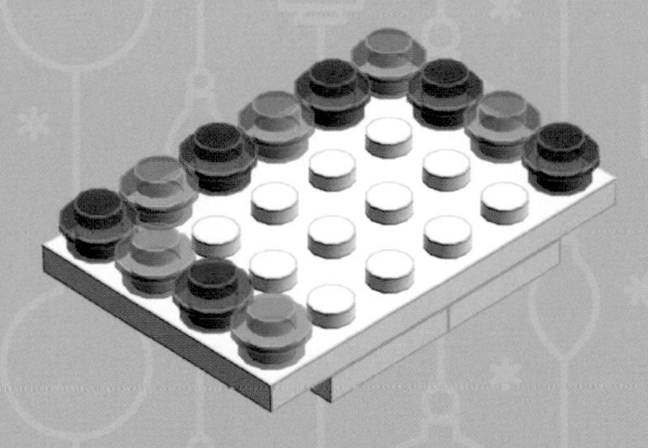

26

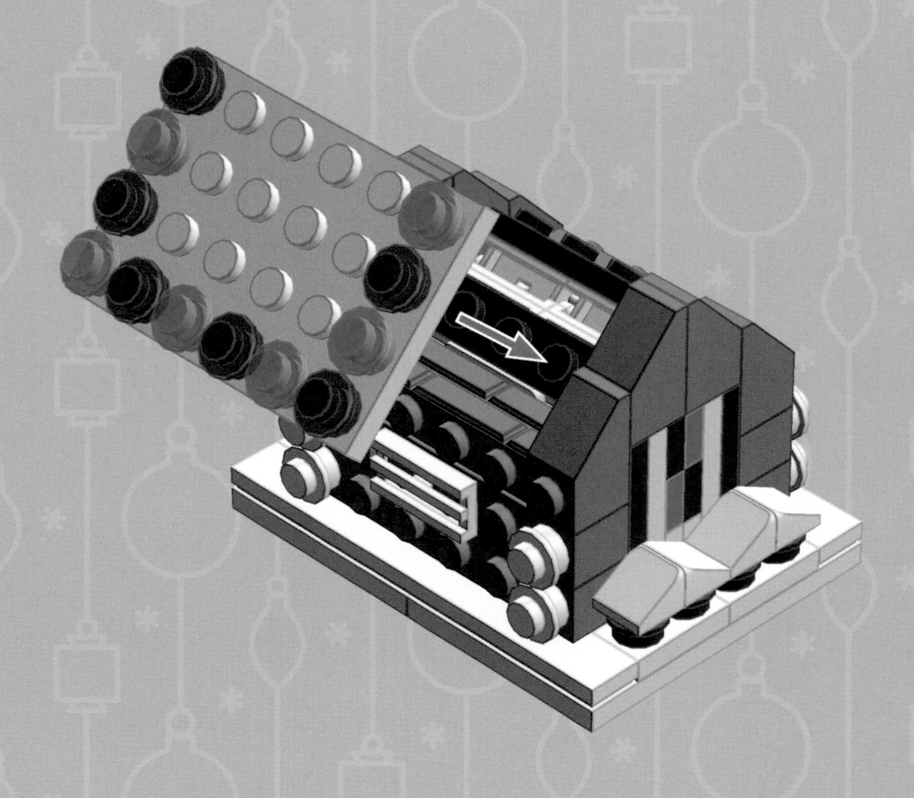

27

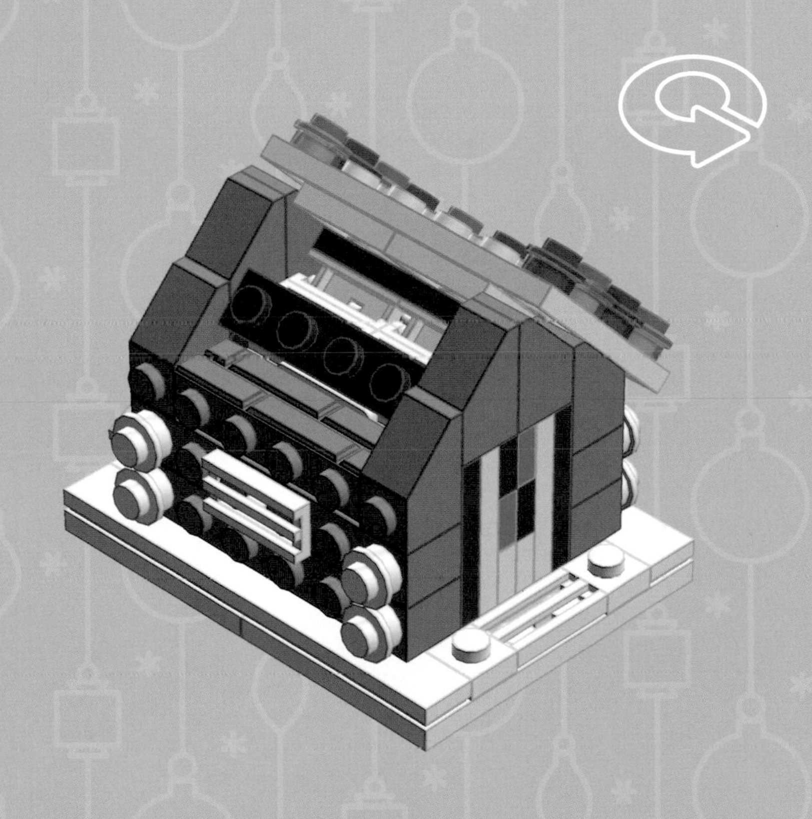

28

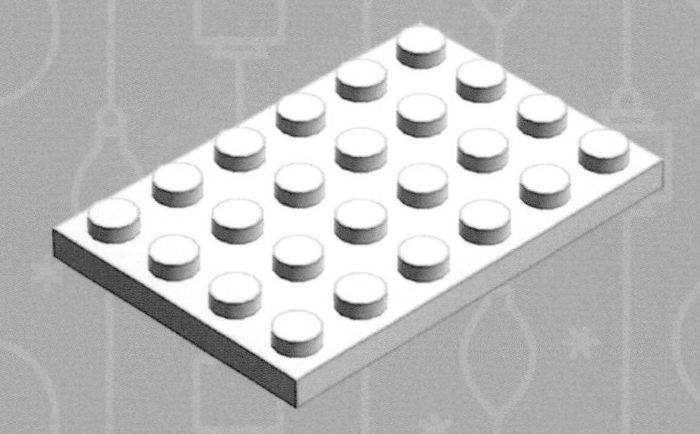

29

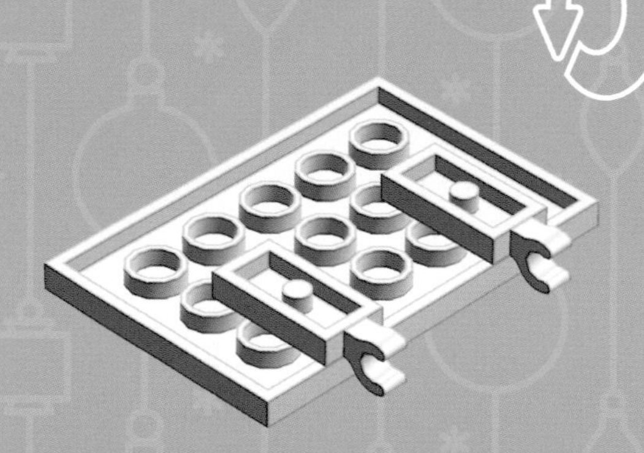

30

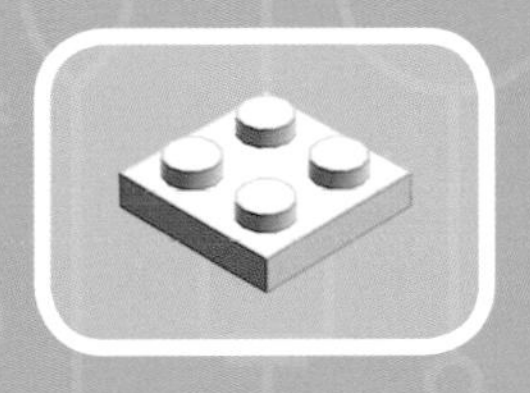

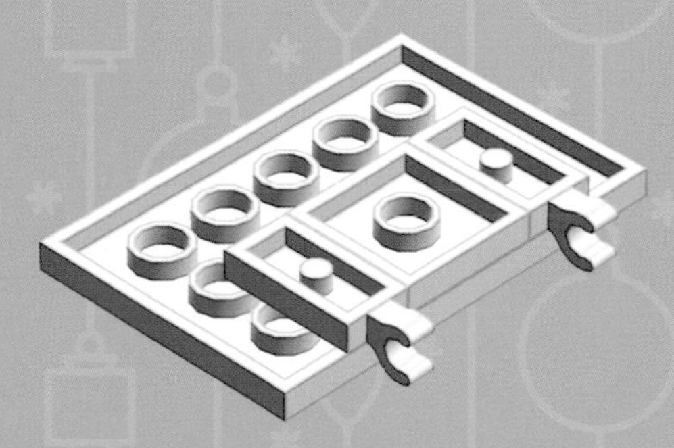

31

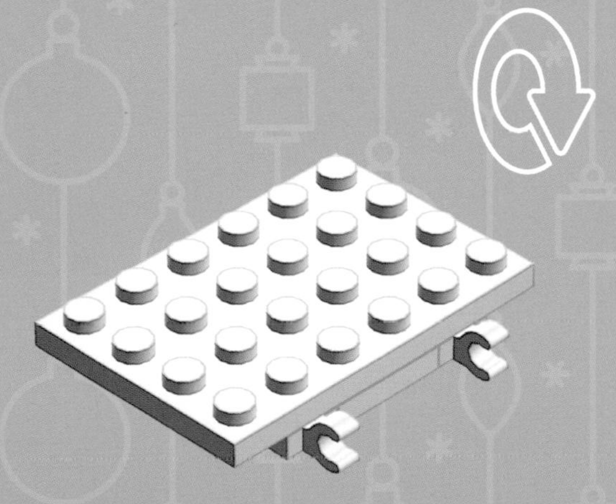

32

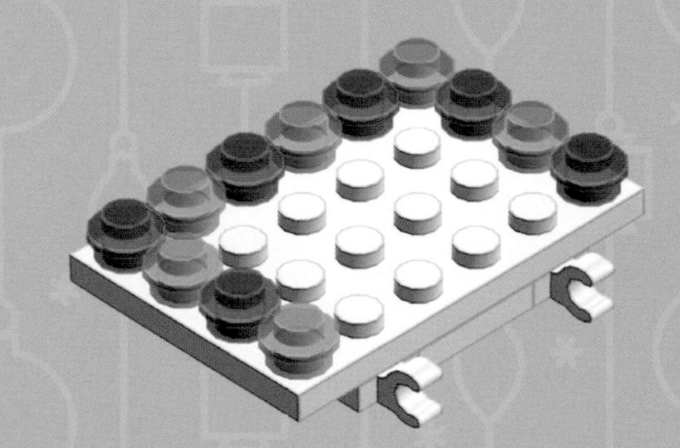

33

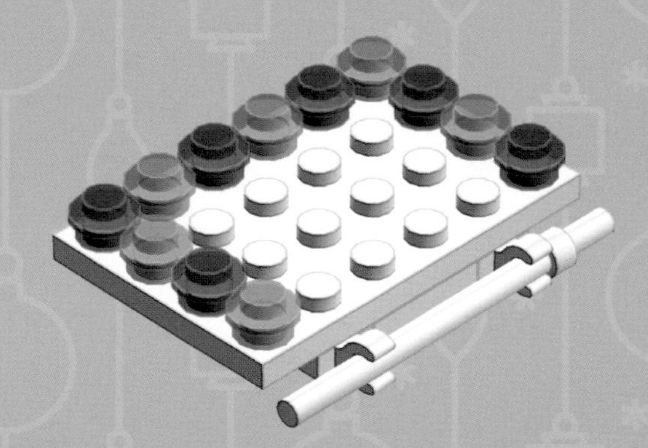

34

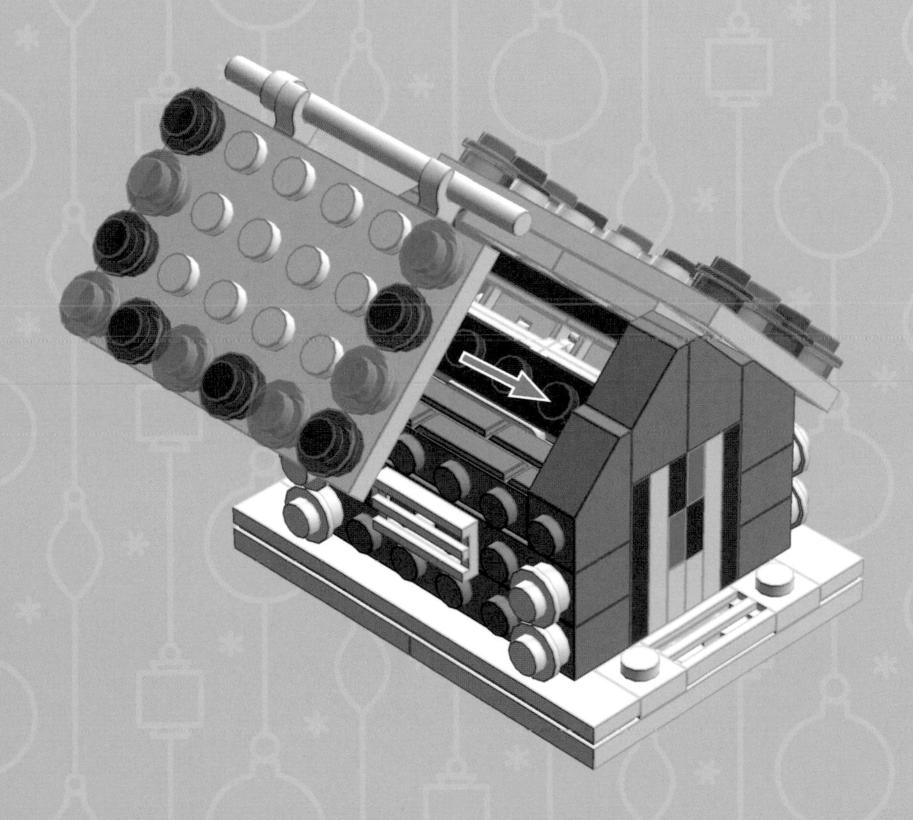

35

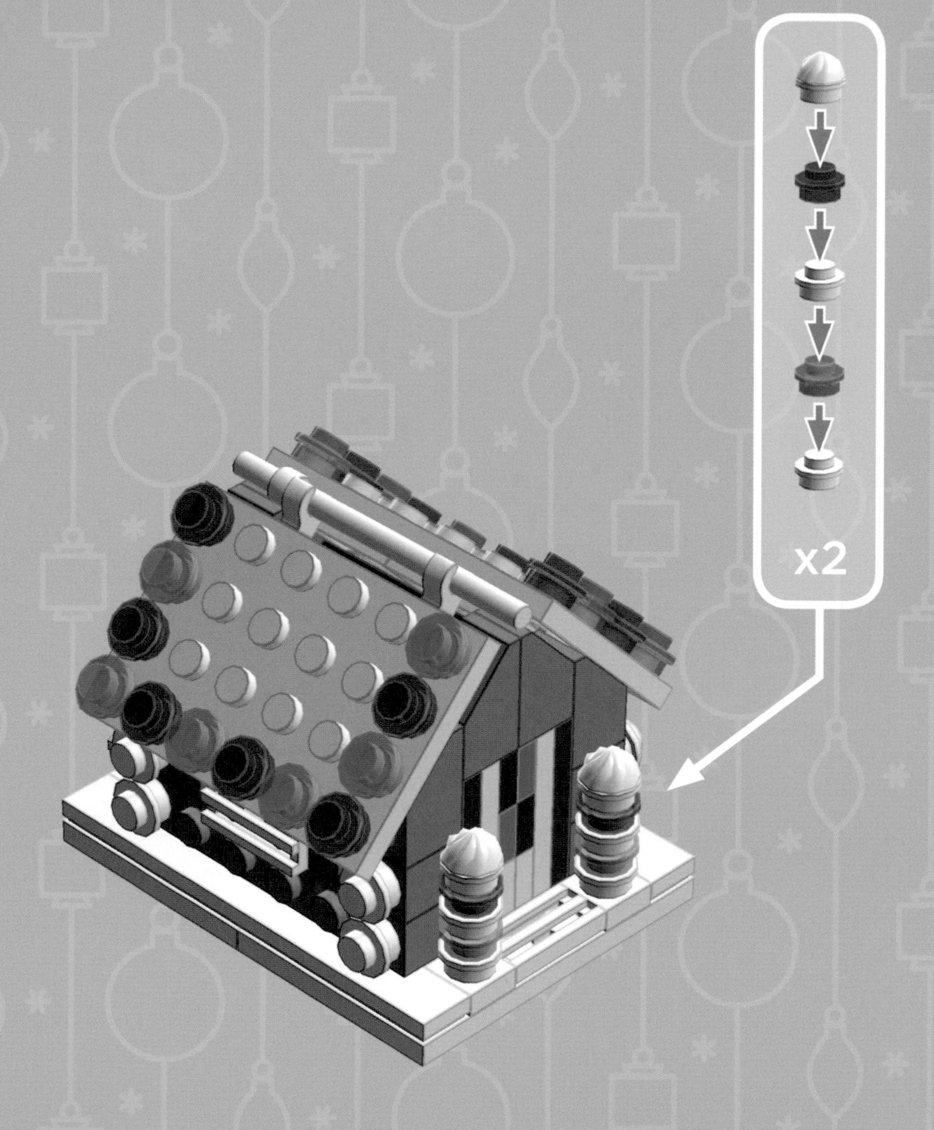

36

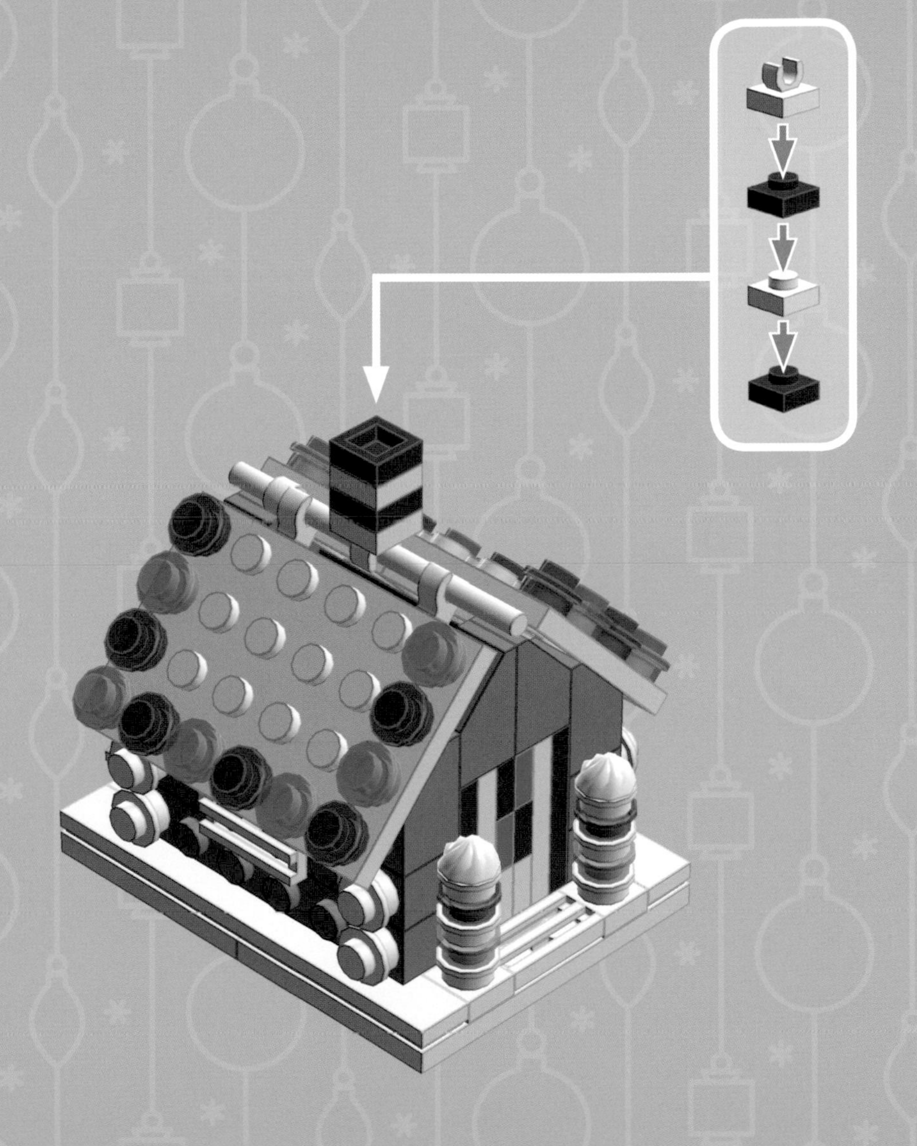

37

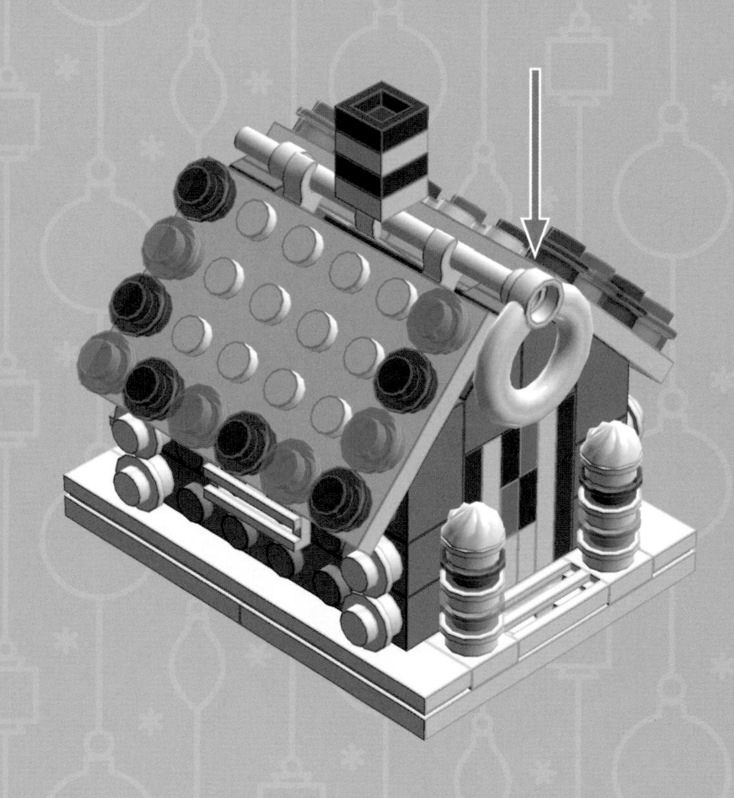

Barrel

6x
4646844

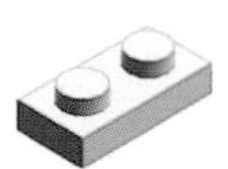

12x
302301

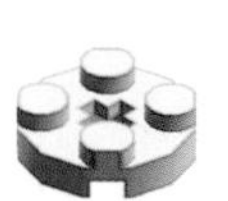

2x
403201

2x
396001

1x
4211622

12x
4518400

4x
4502595

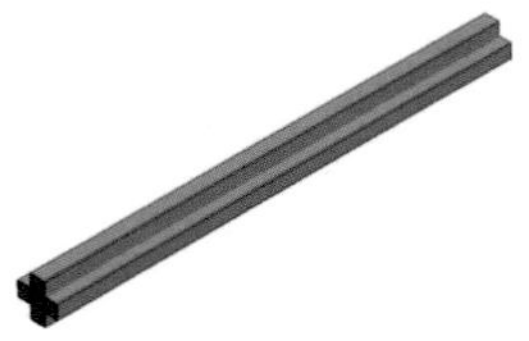

1x
4211805

6x
4581308

6x
4565324

1x
6010831

6x
379521

1

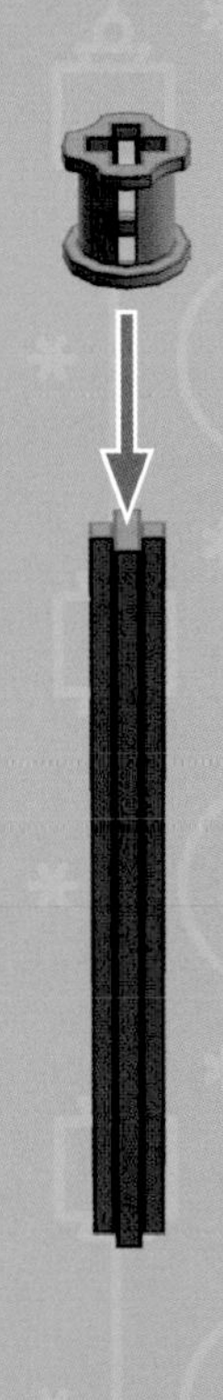

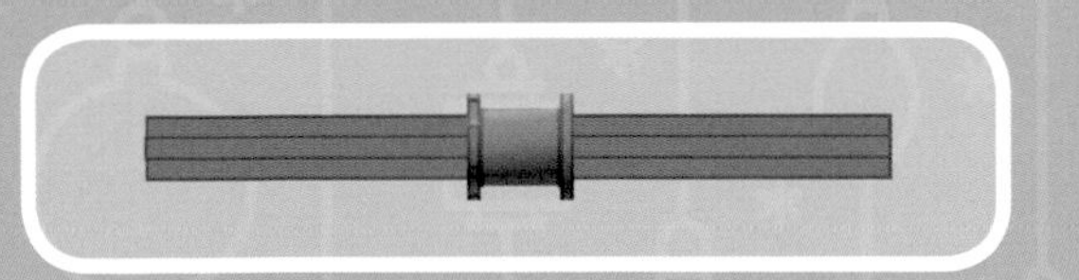

2

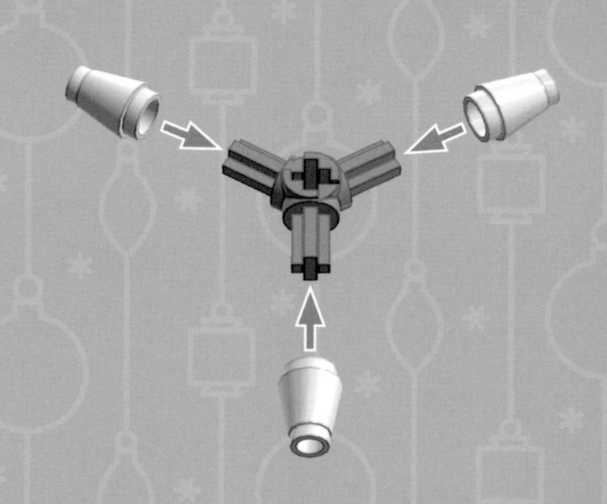

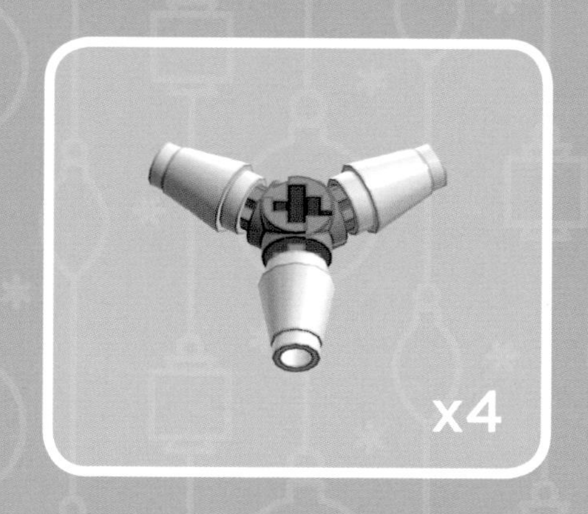

3

4

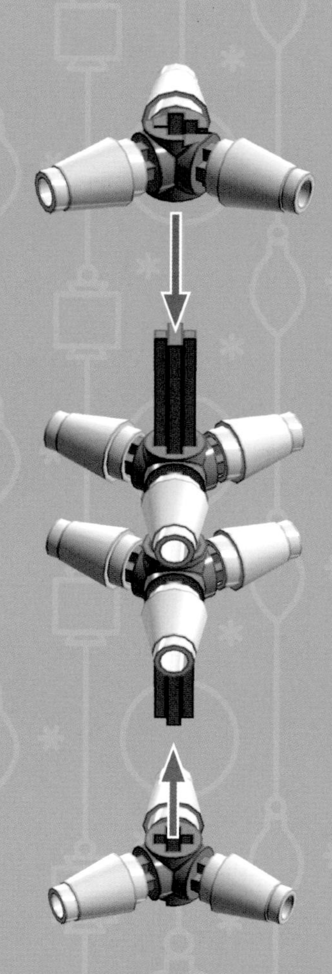

5

6

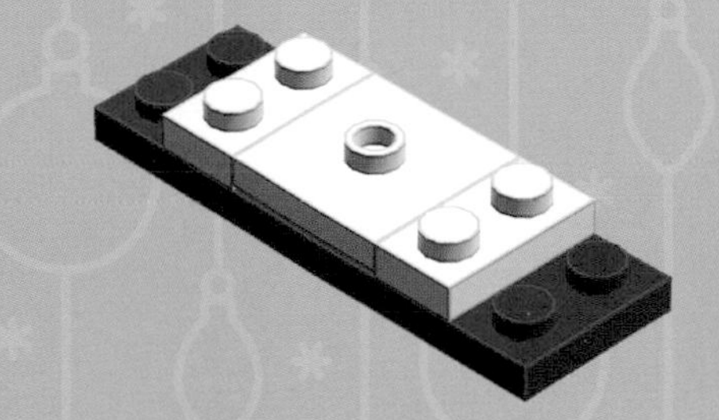

7

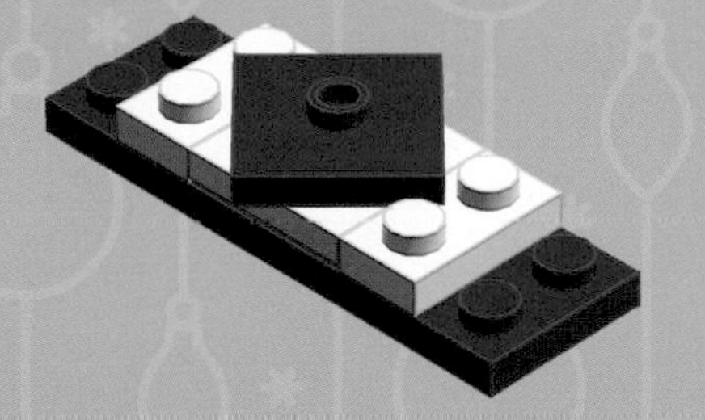

8

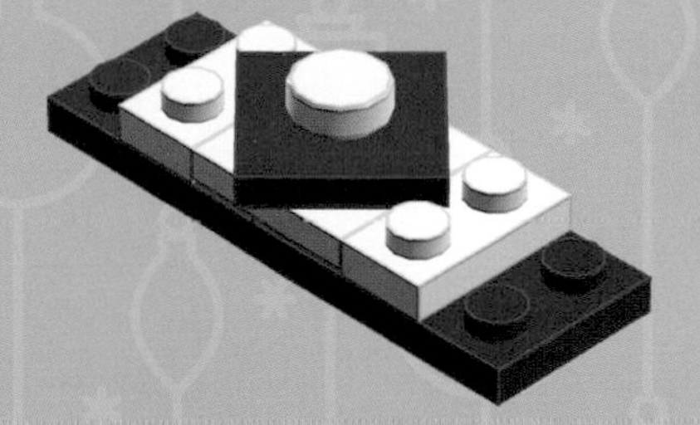

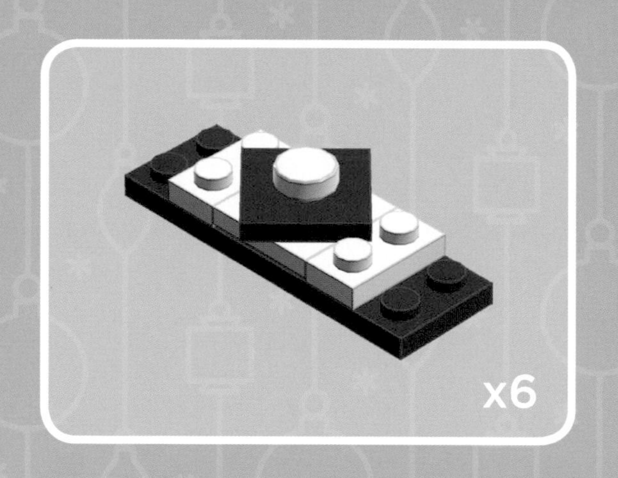
x6

9

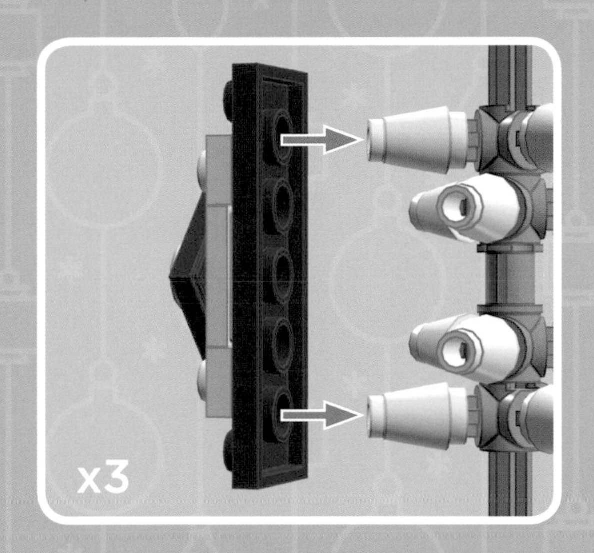

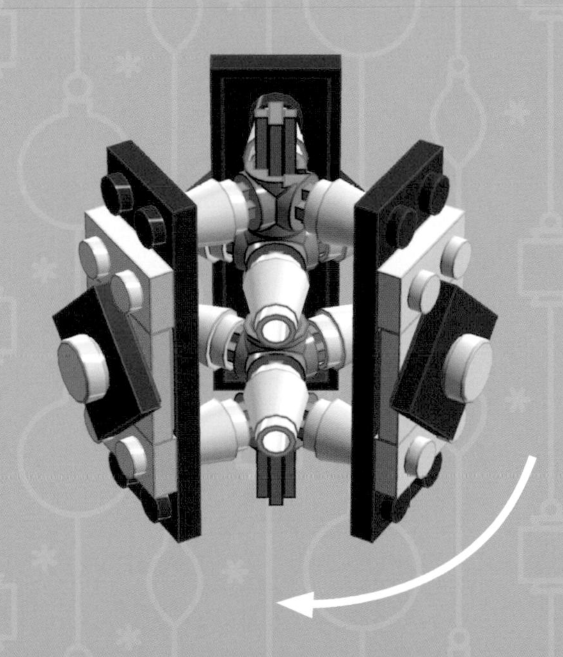

10

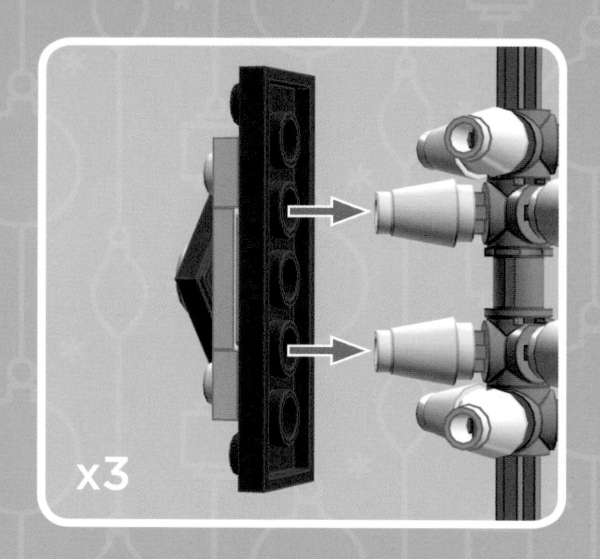

11

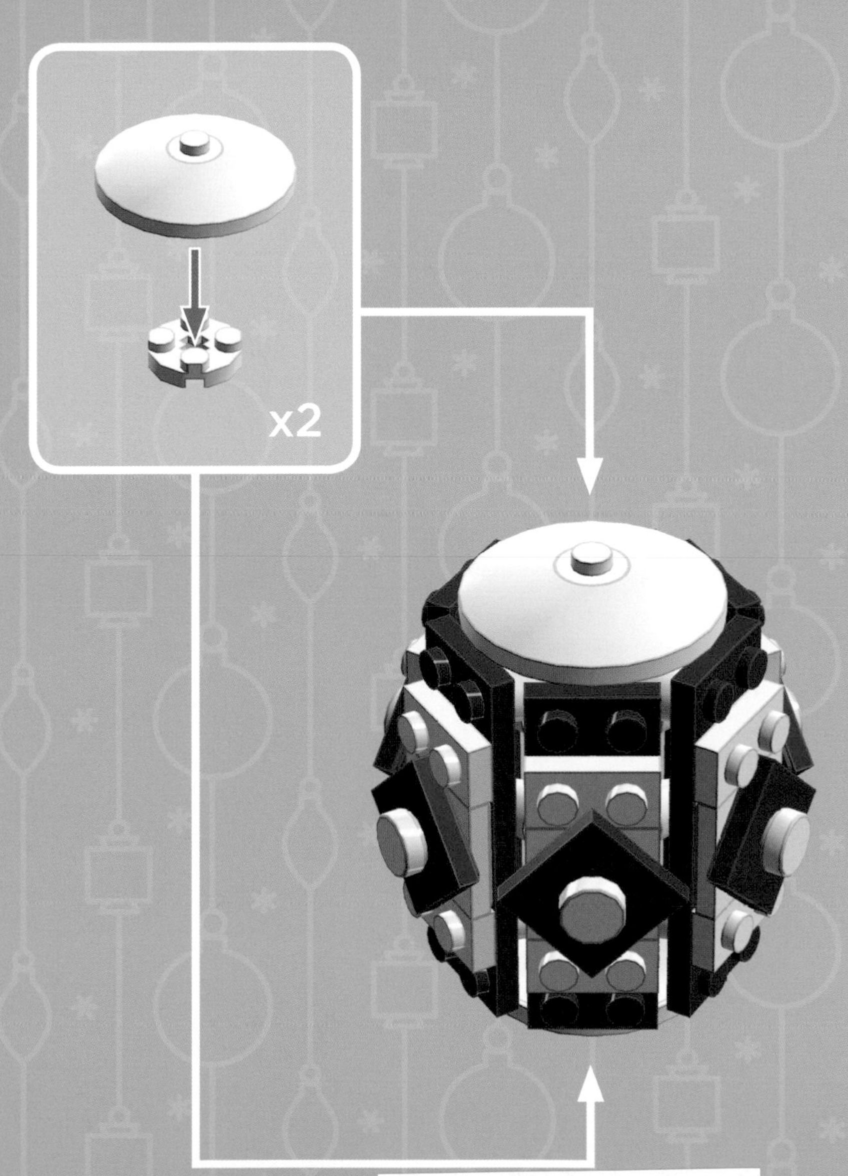

12

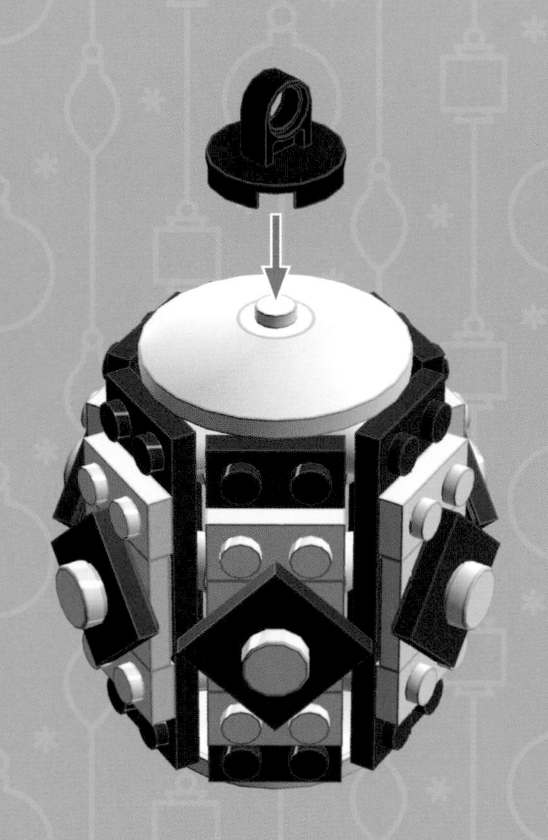

Ball

1x
6010831

12x
6000071

12x
4651524

4x
4502595

1x
4211622

12x
4518400

2x
403201

12x
4249506

2x
396001

6x
302028

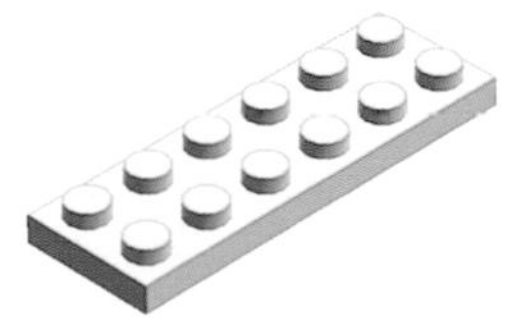

6x
379501

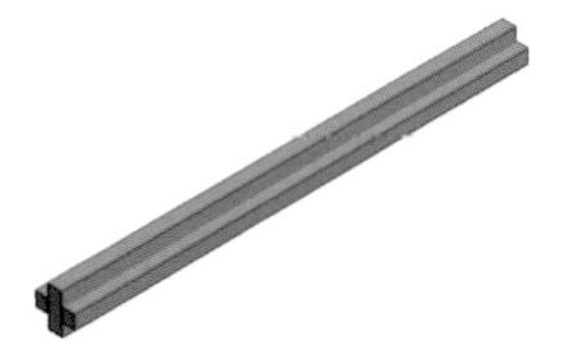

1x
4211805

1

2

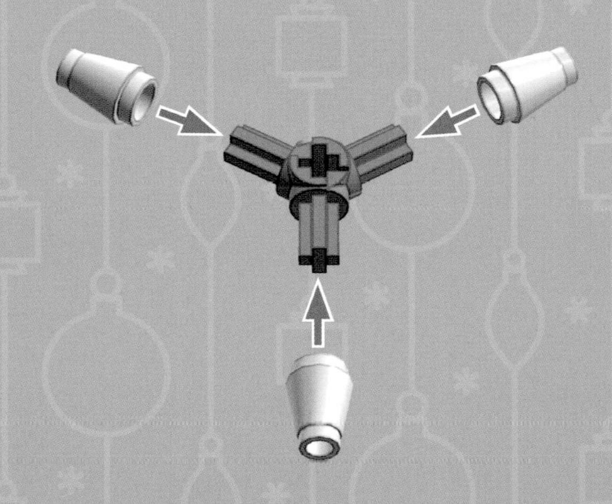

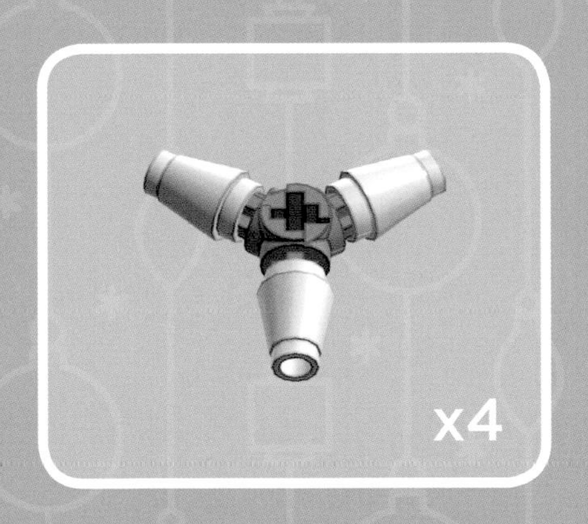

3

4

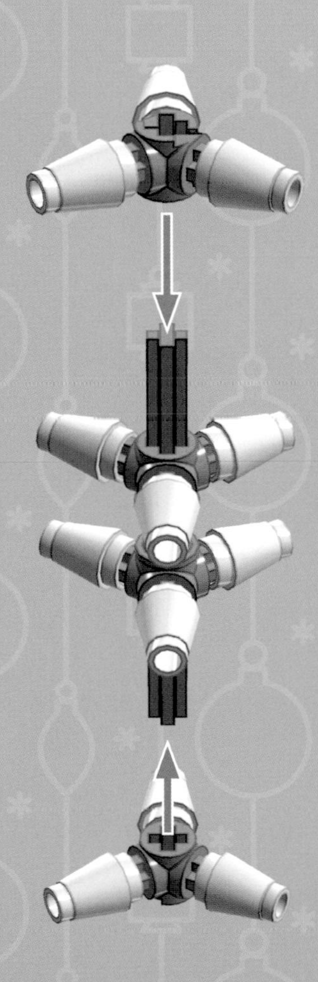

5

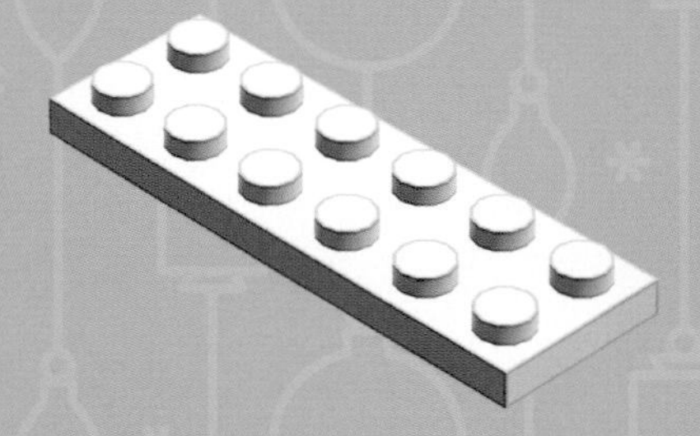

6

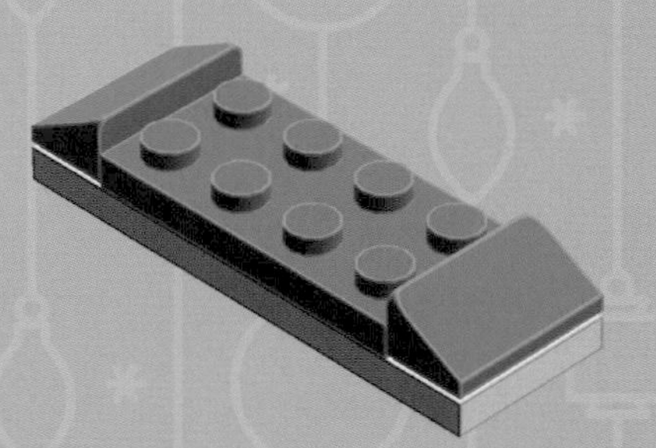

7

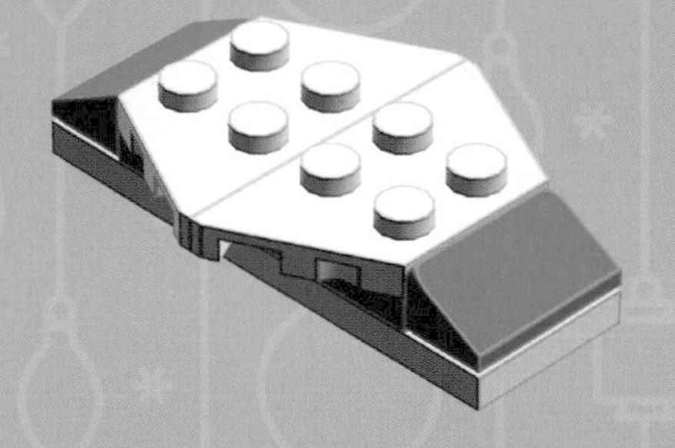

8

x3

9

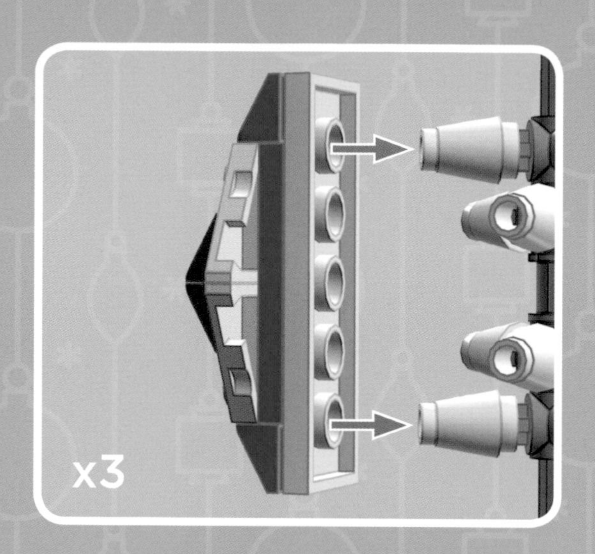

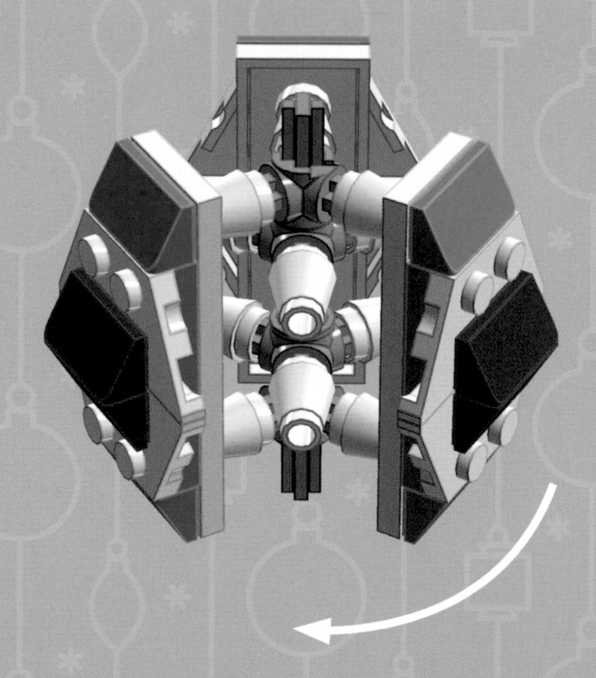

10

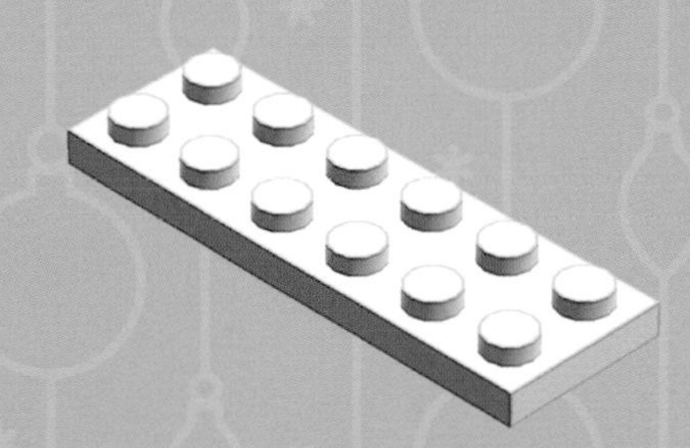

11

12

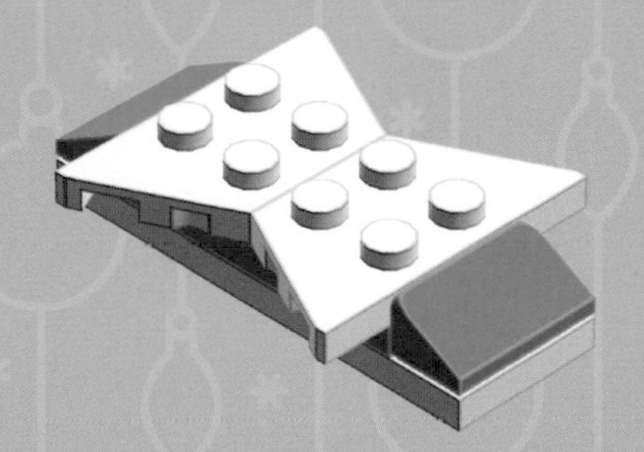

13

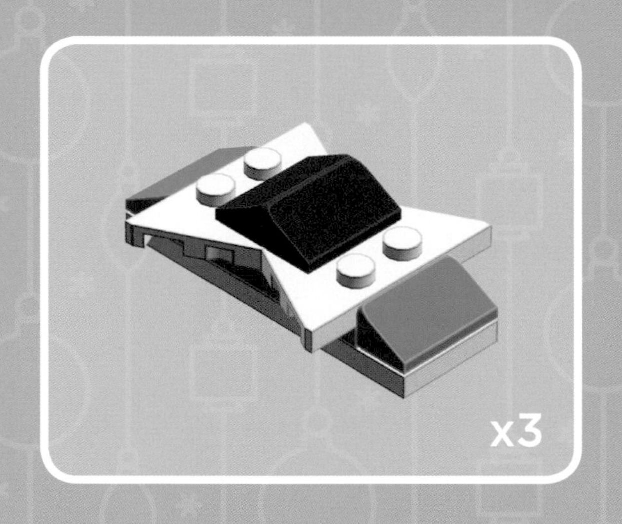
x3

14

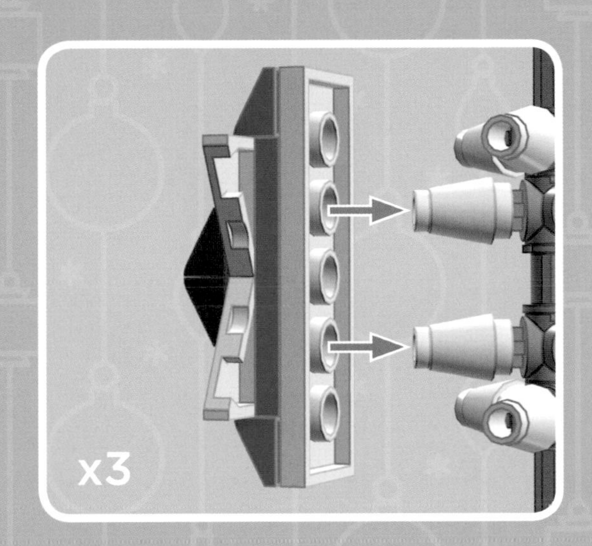

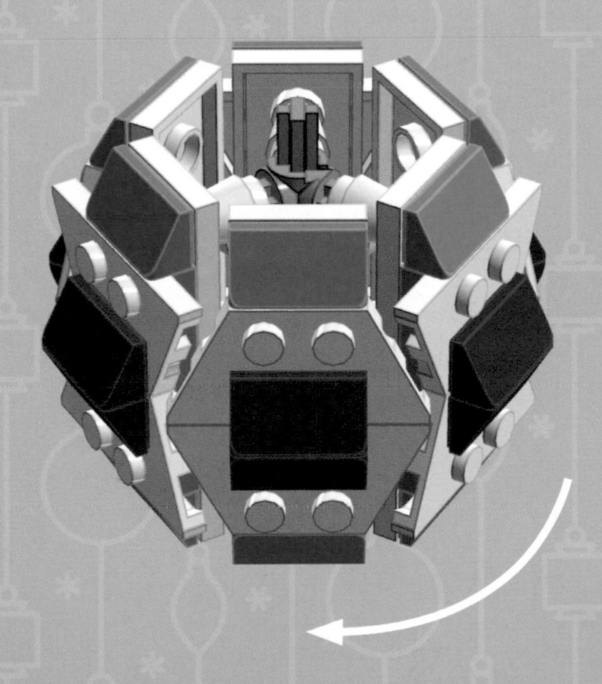

15

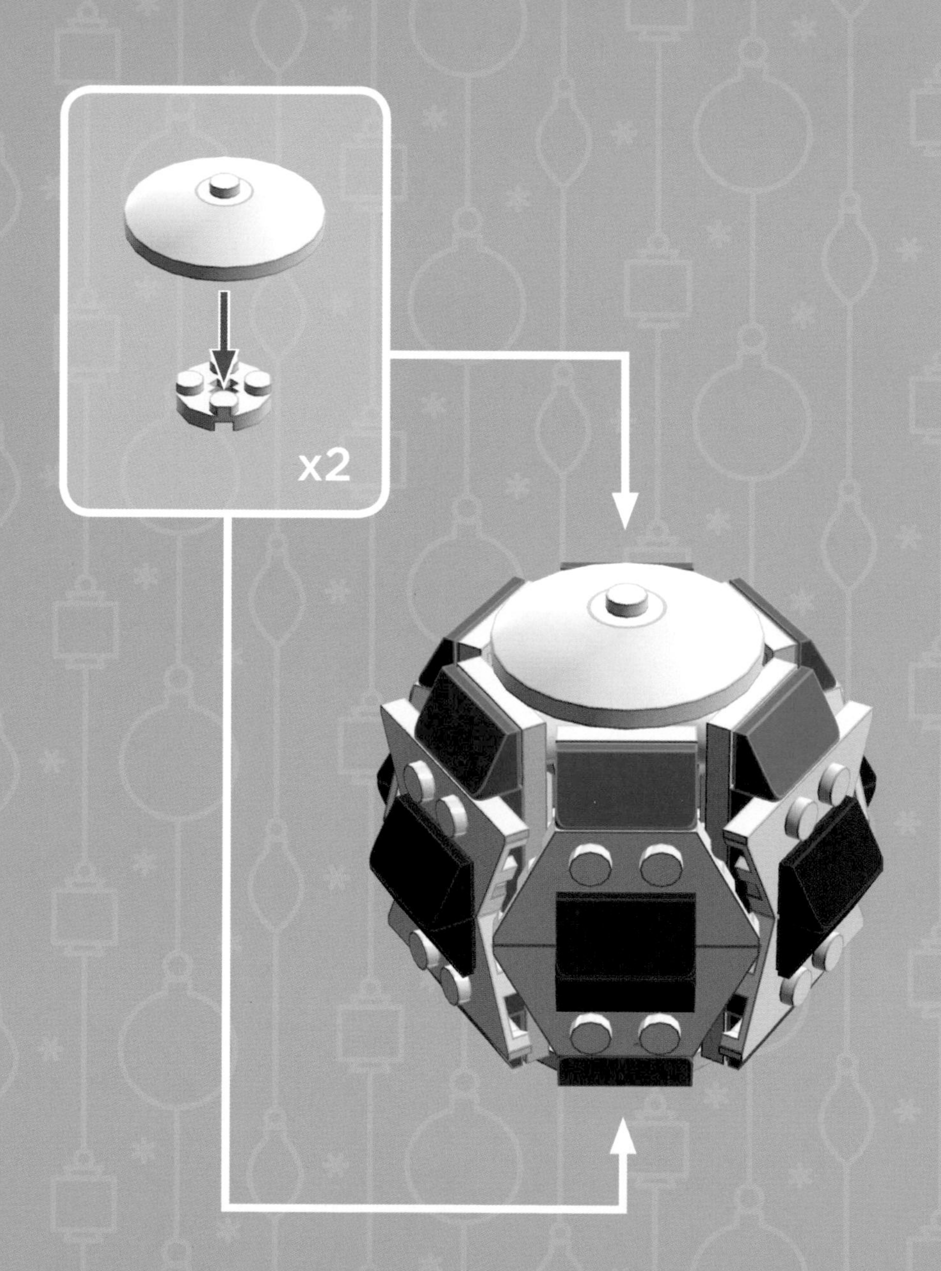

16

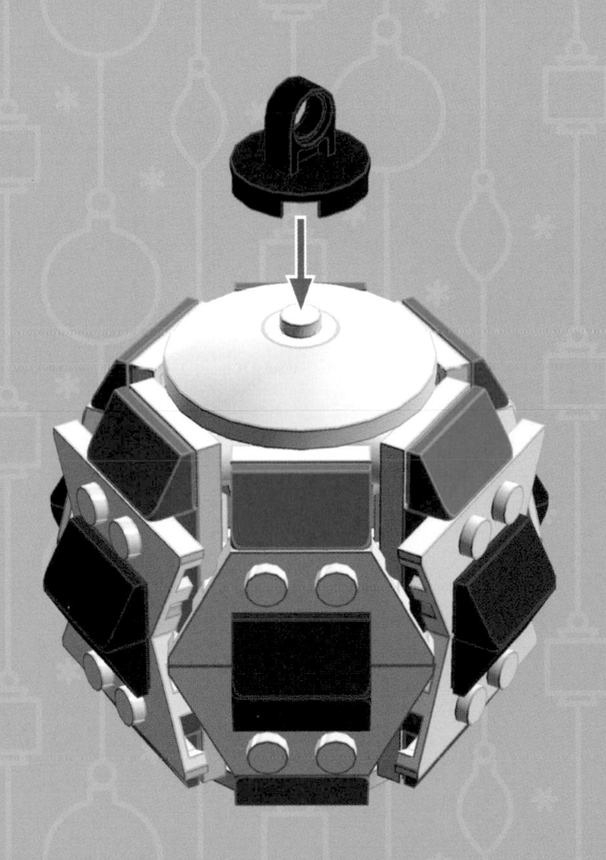

Flip the green slopes for a different look!

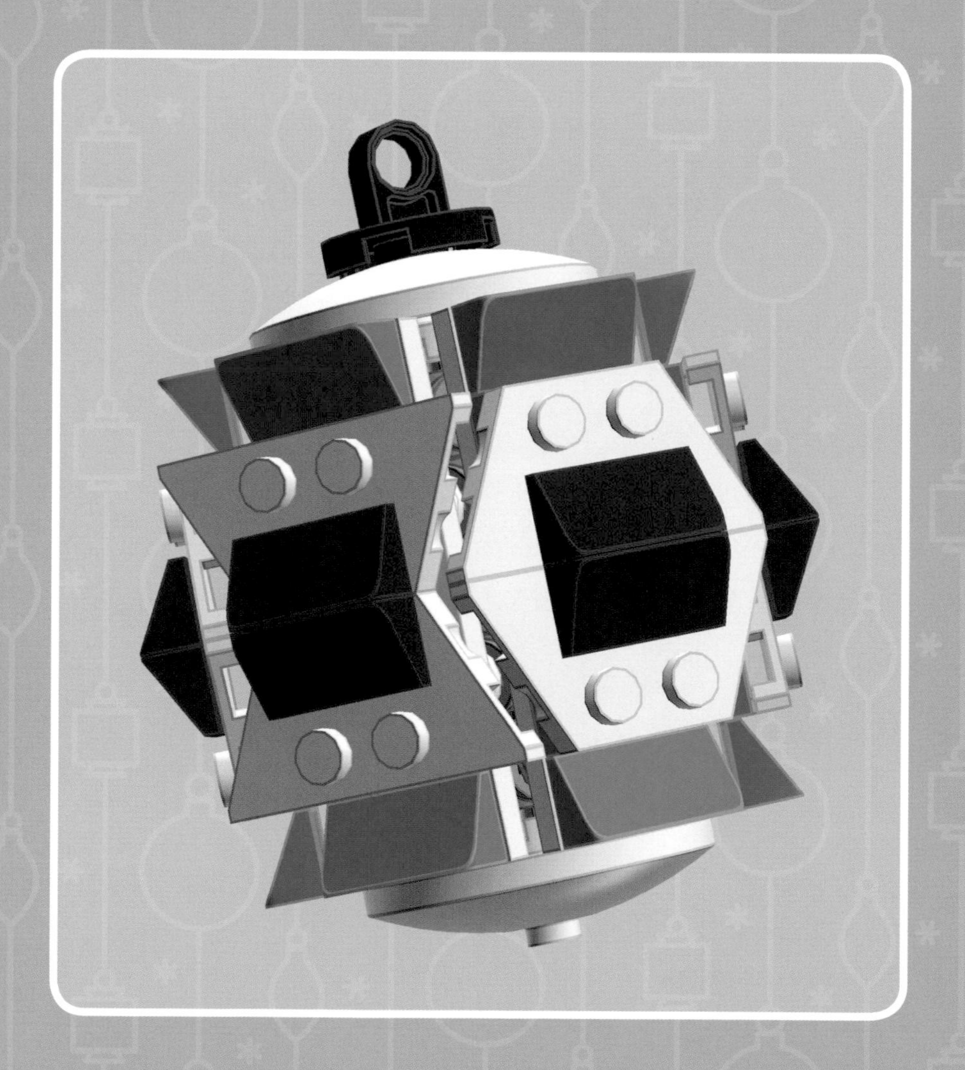

Bow

1x
6103444

6x
4651524

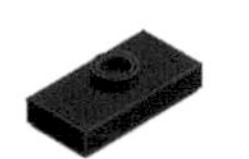
3x
6092565

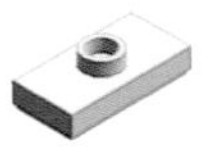
12x
6051511

6x
4249563

2x
4518400

3x
6044691

6x
6105976

6x
6000752

3x
302121

6x
302001

3x
370901

3x
4527839

6x
243101

1x
4502595

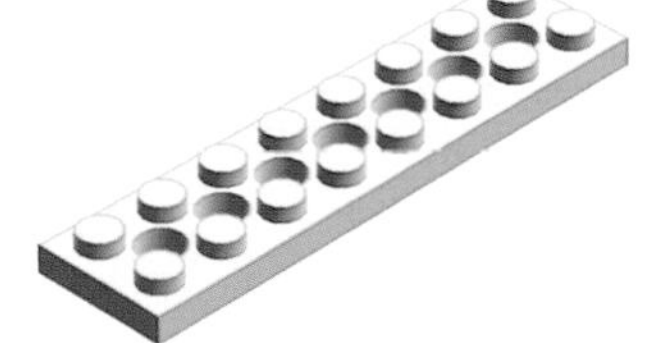
3x
4527945

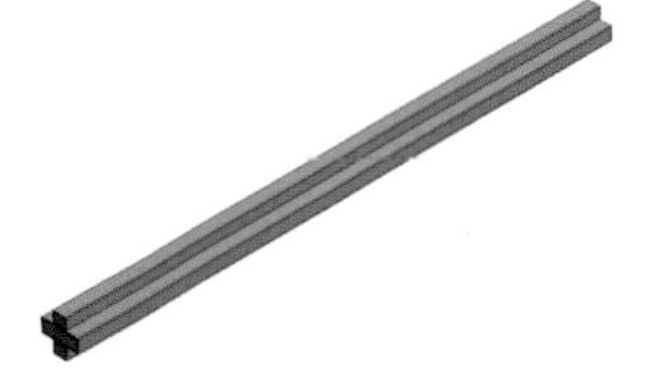
1x
4535768

1

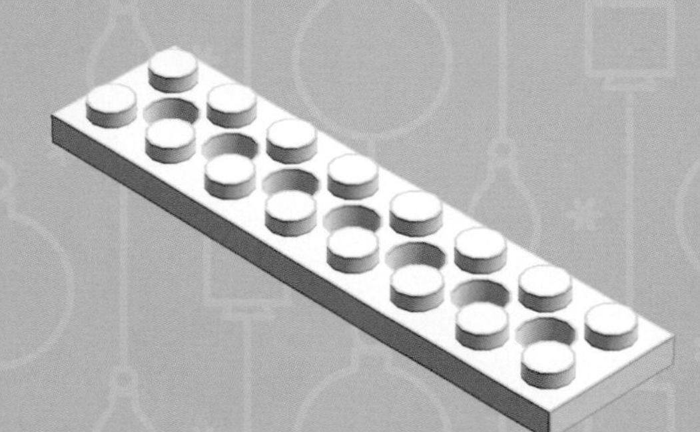

2

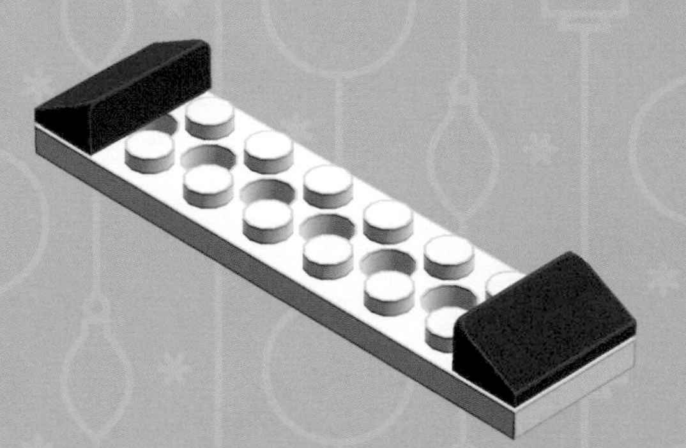

3

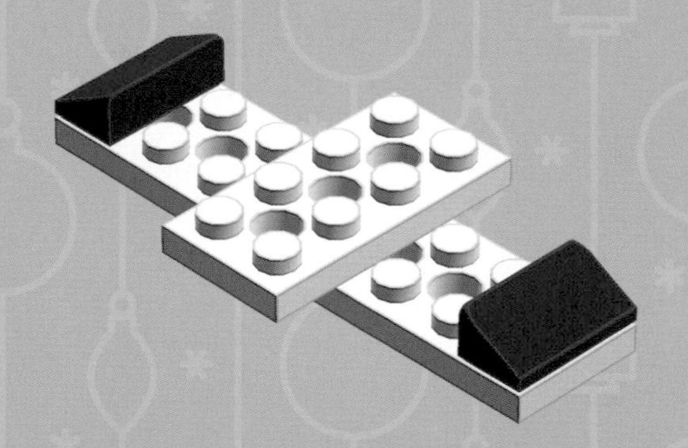

4

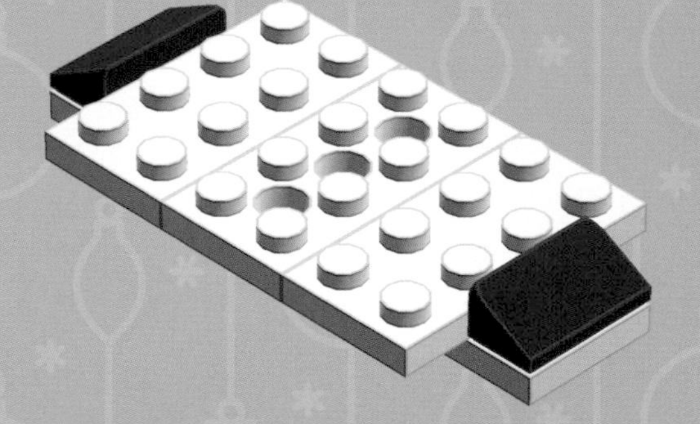

5

6

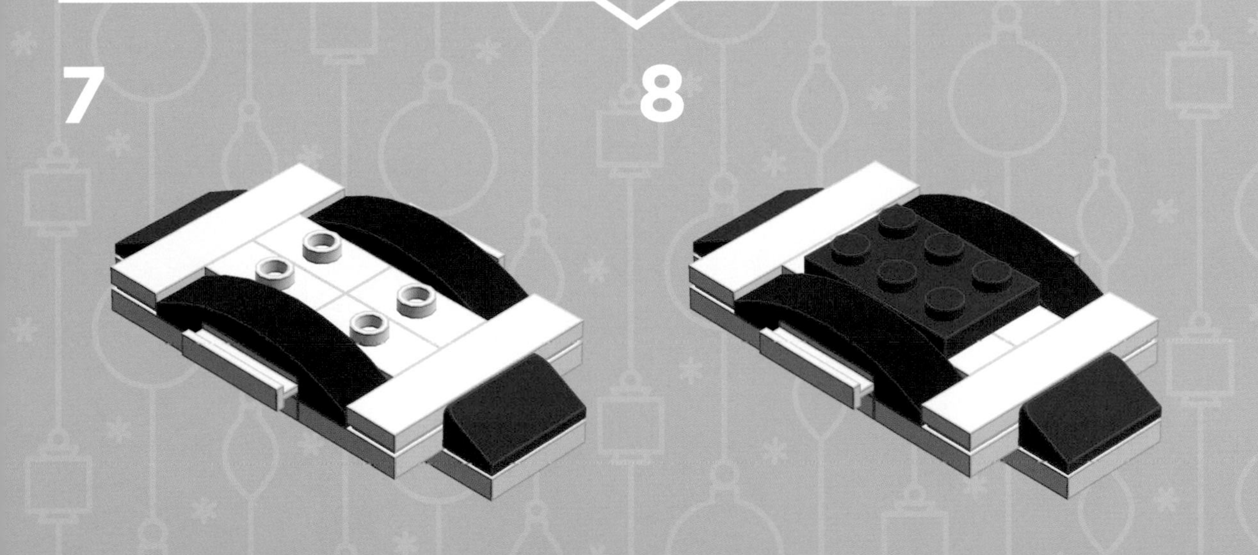

9

10

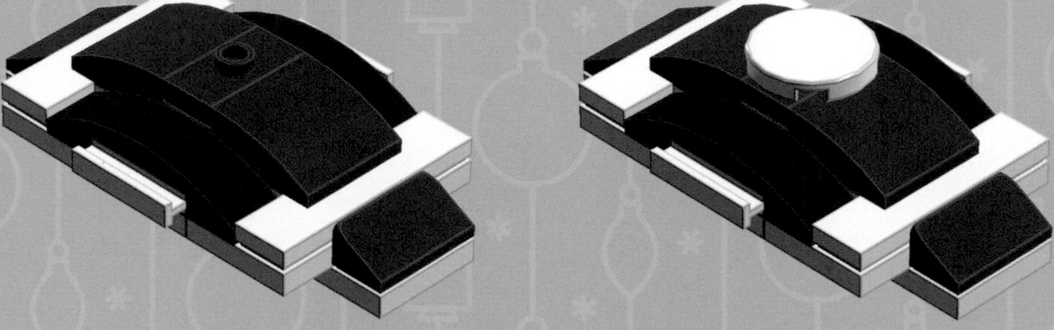

11

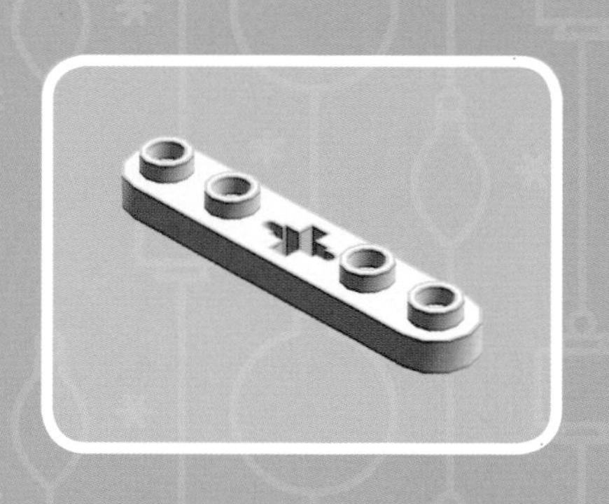

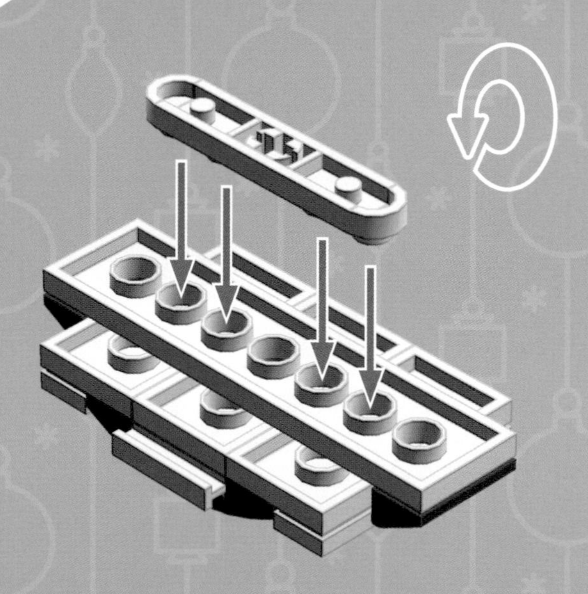

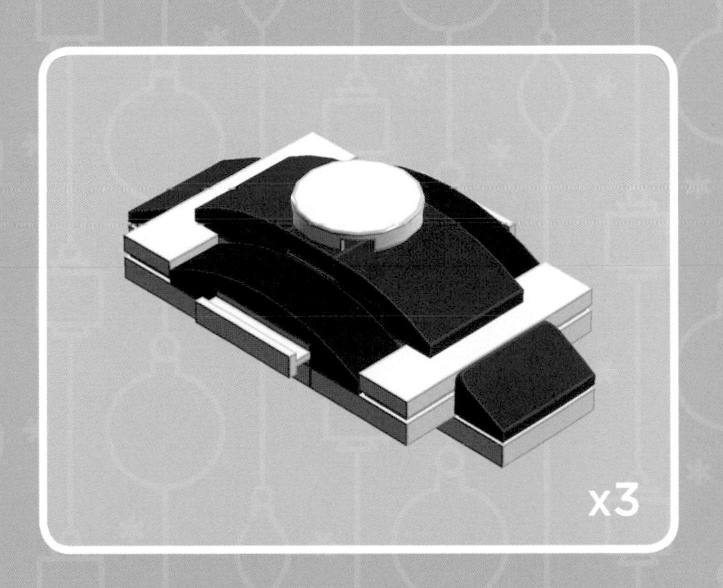
x3

12

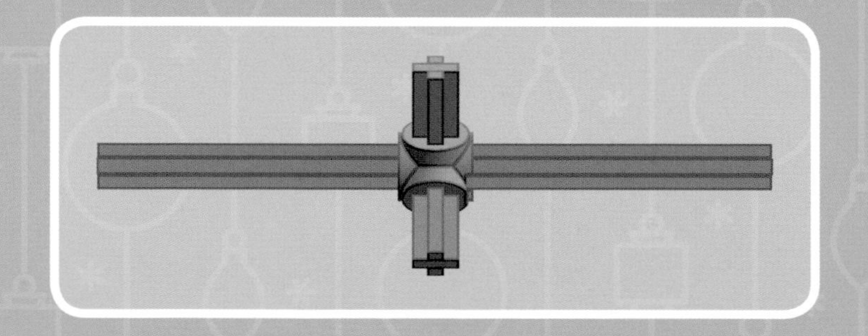

13

14

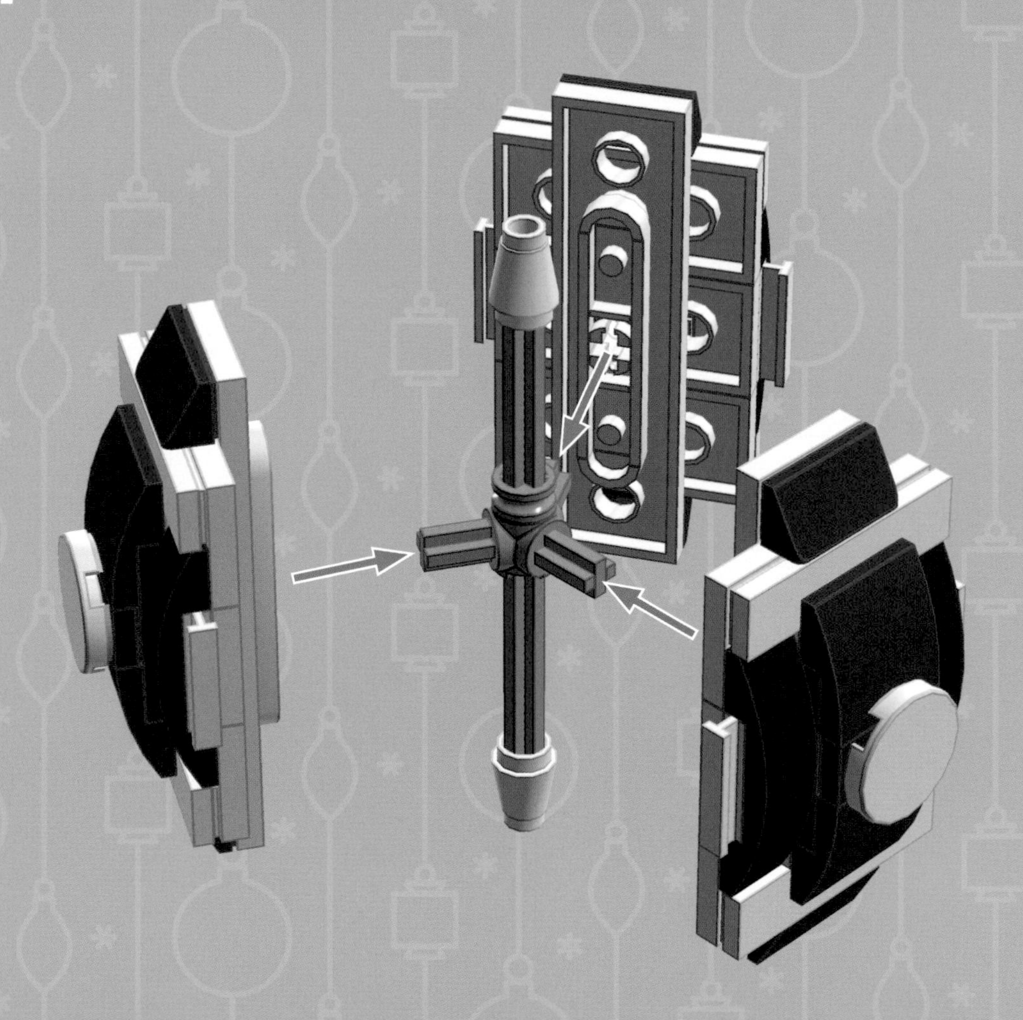

15

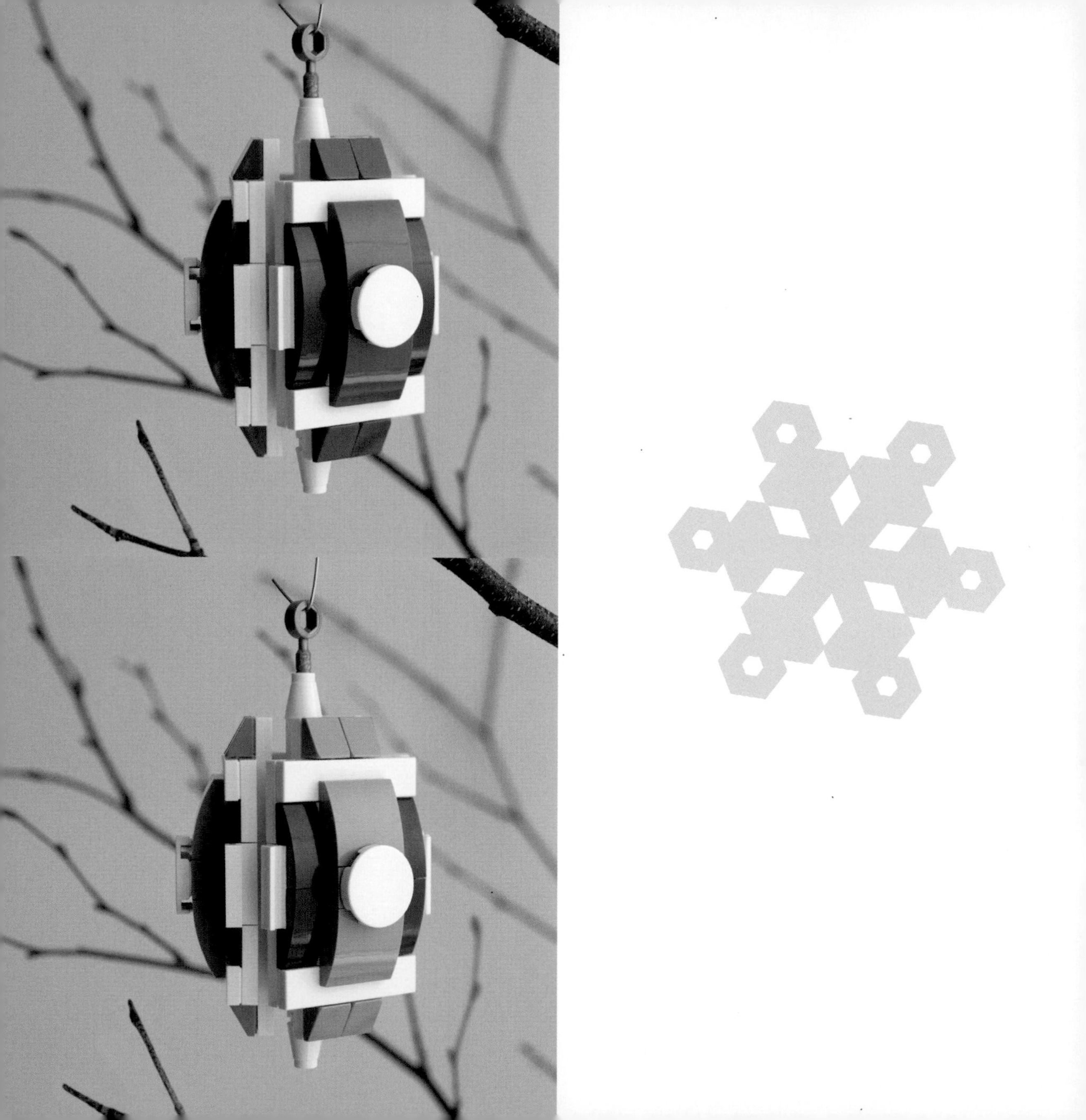

Frill

1x
6103444

12x
6094137

12x
4504372

2x
4518400

6x
6025026

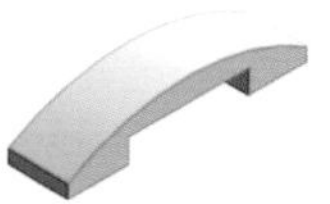

6x
6023806

1x
4502595

3x
4537936

3x
370901

3x
4527947

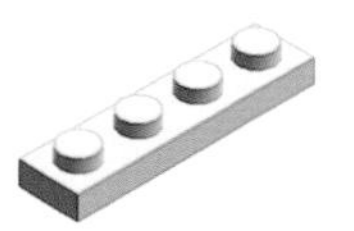

6x
371001

3x
4527839

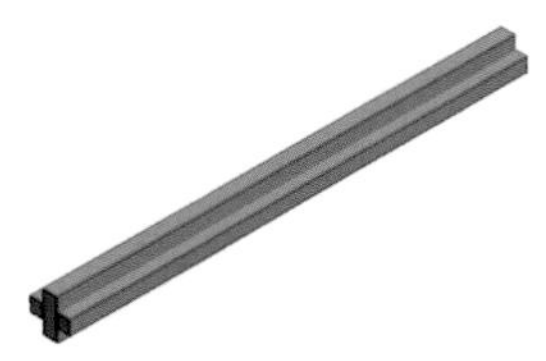

1x
4211805

1

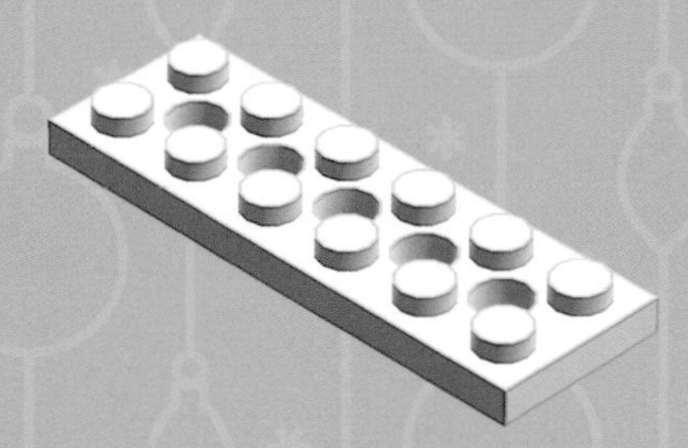

2

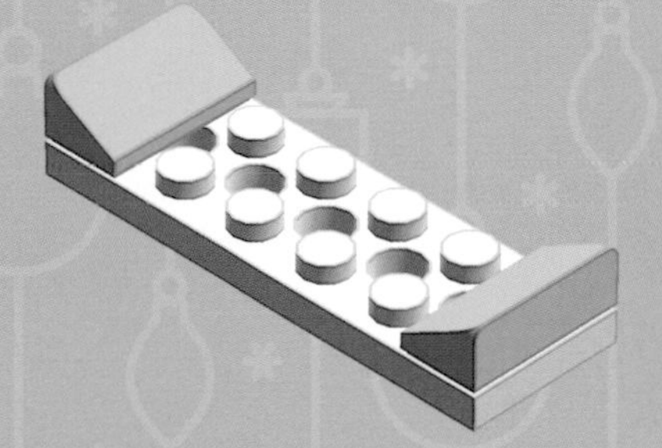

3

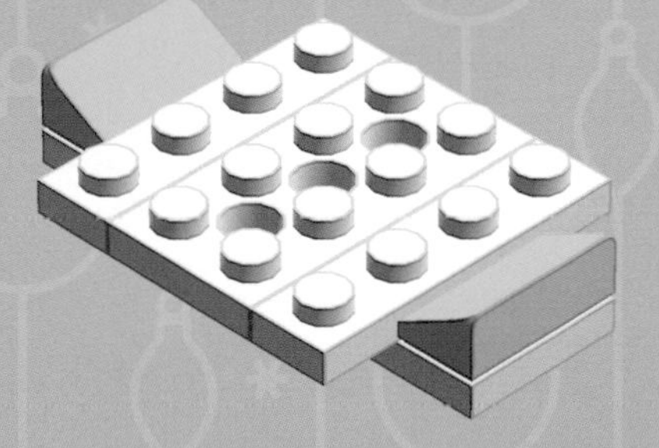

4

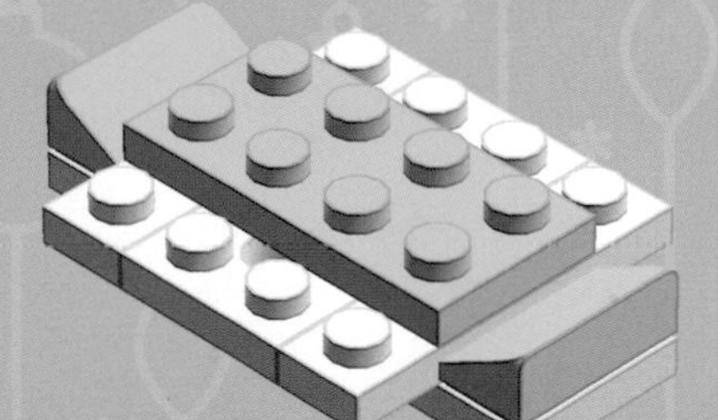

5

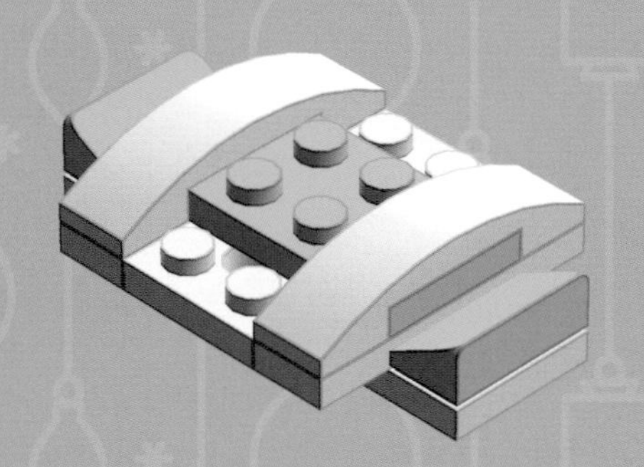

6

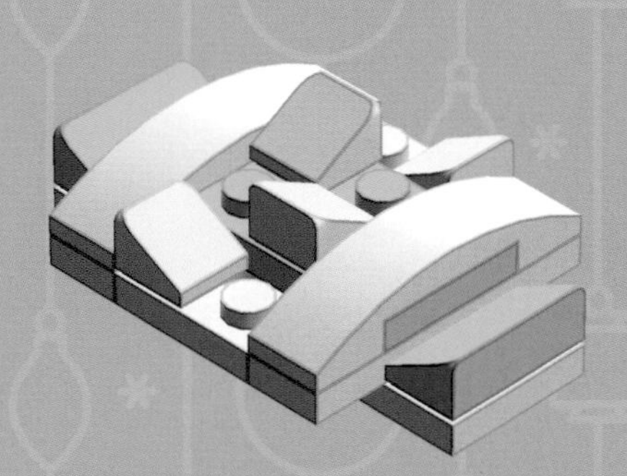

7

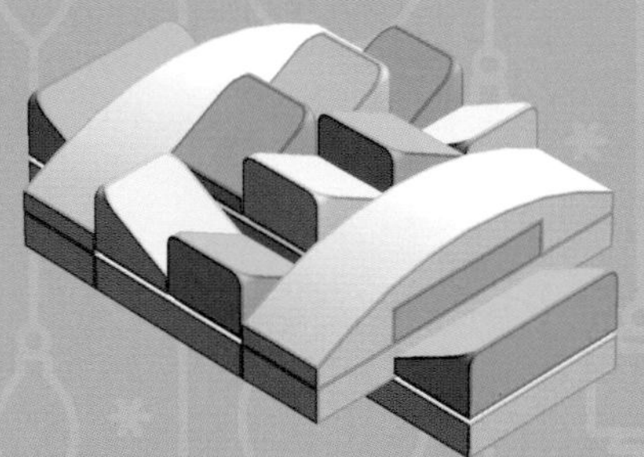

8

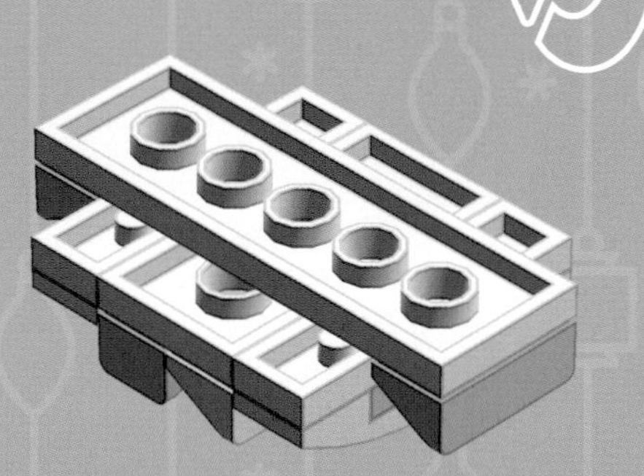

9

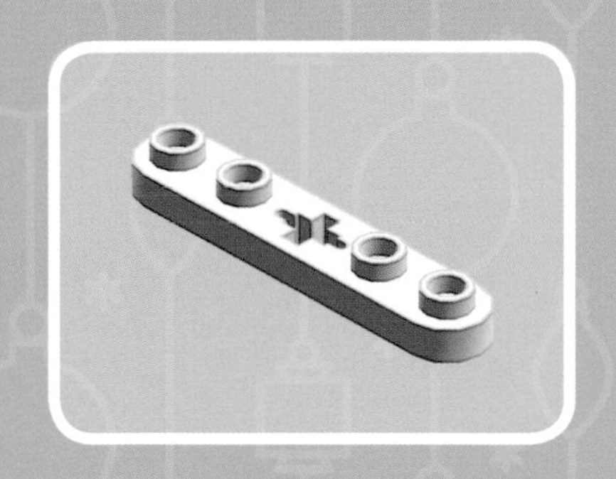

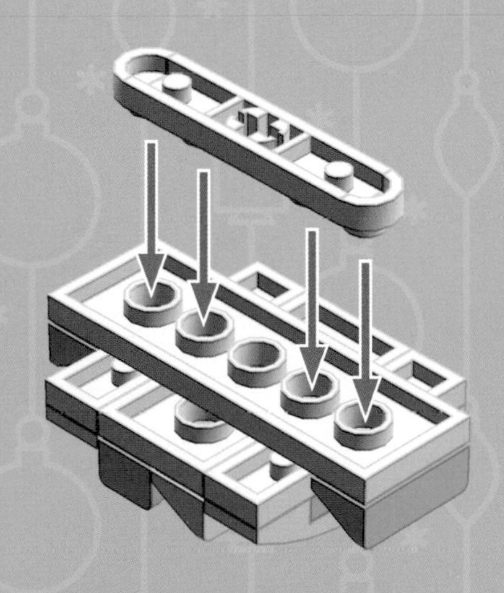

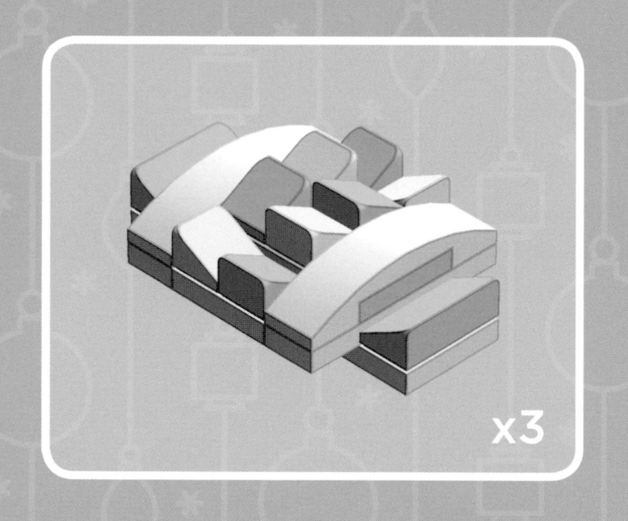
x3

10

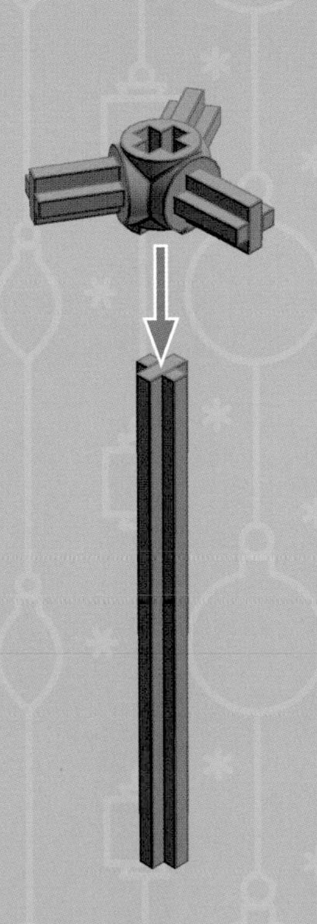

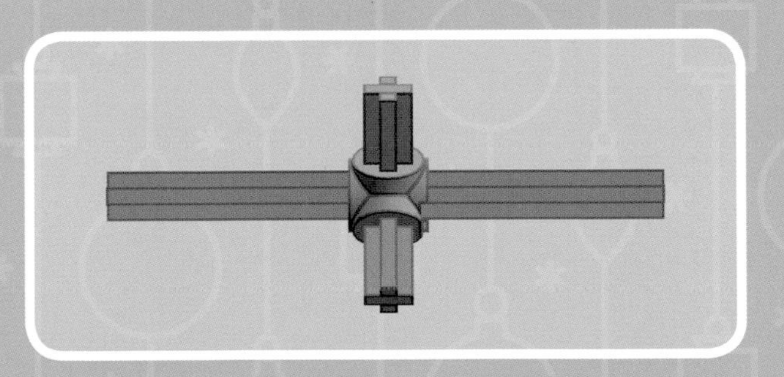

11

12

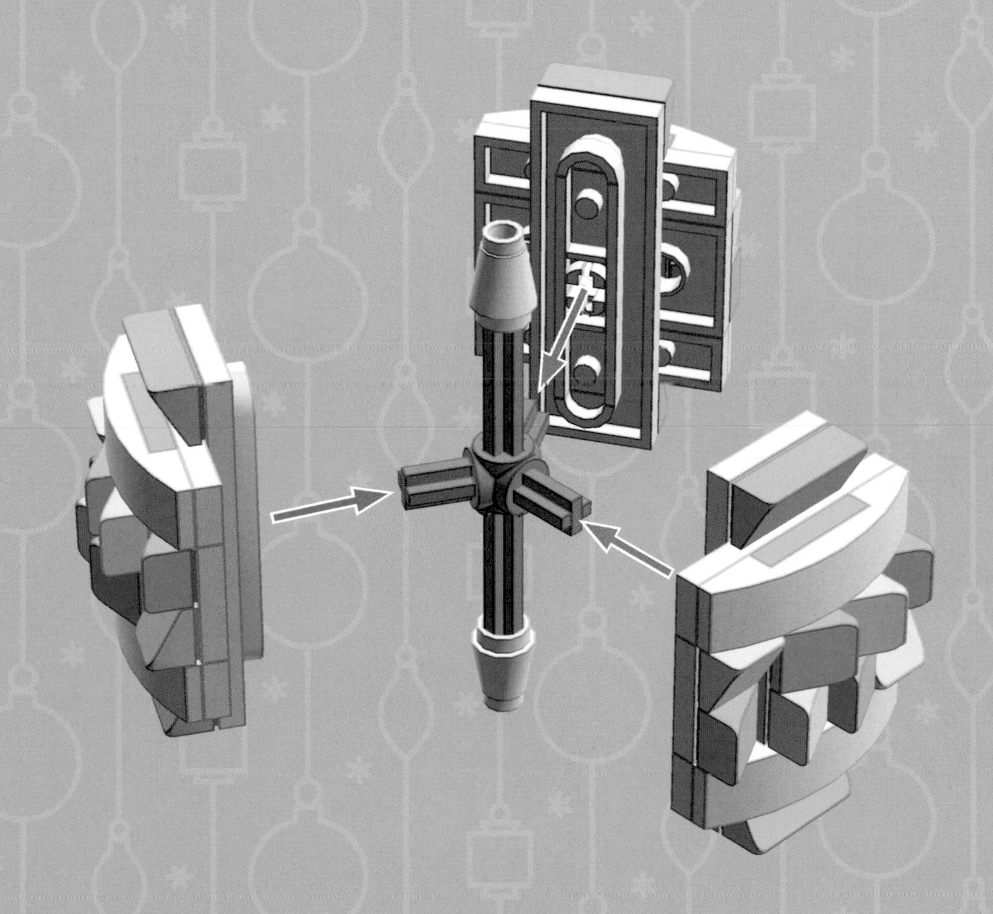

13

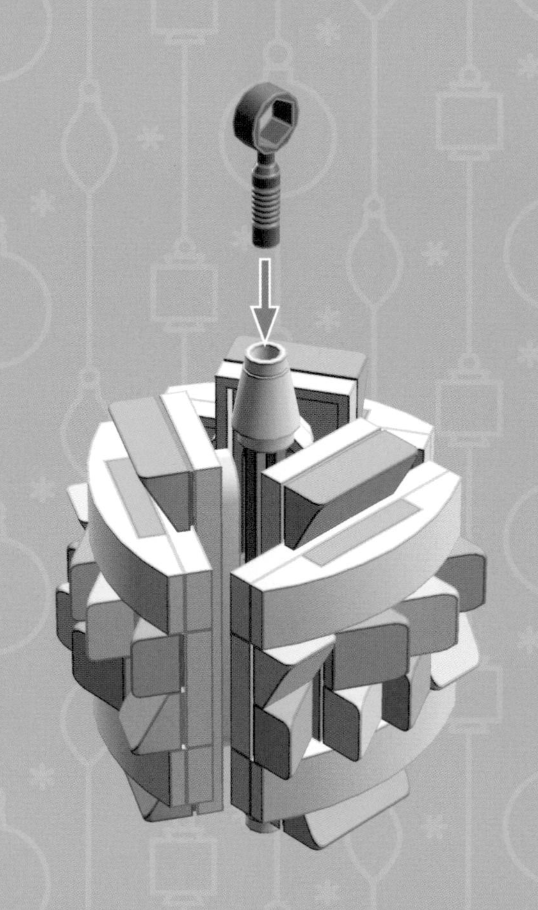

Lantern

1x
6010831

8x
4651524

8x
6000071

8x
4107762

8x
302228

1x
6013866

4x
4211502

3x
300301

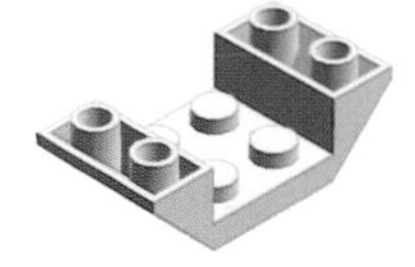

4x
4173943

8x
4249506

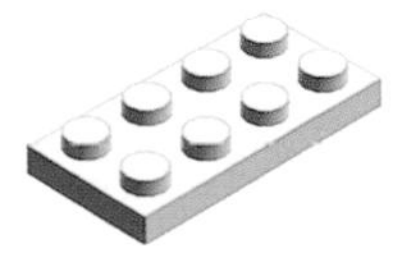

4x
302001

1

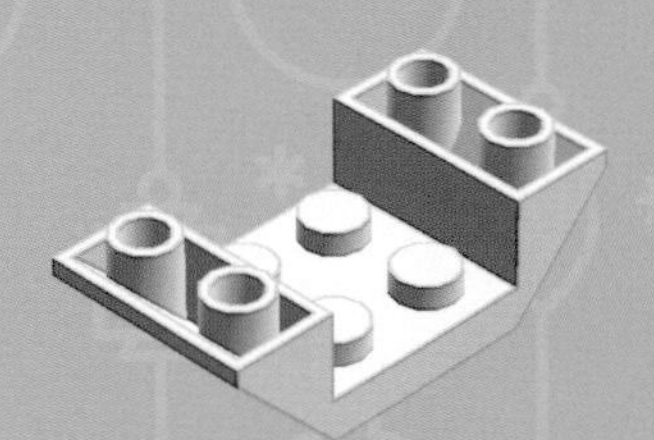

2

3

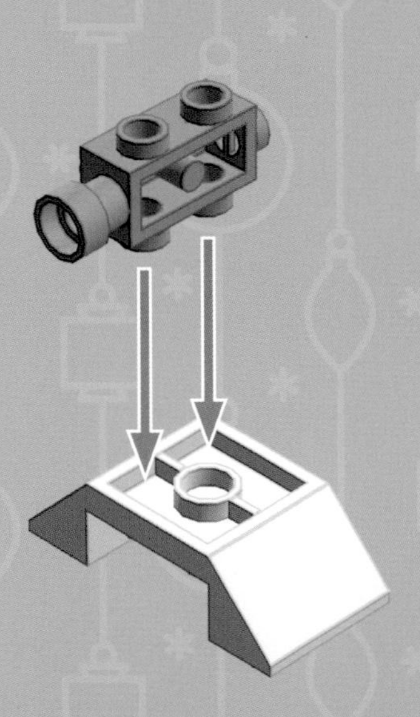

4

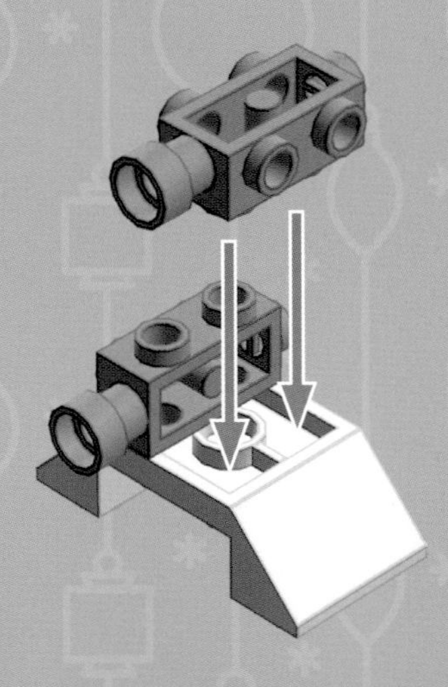

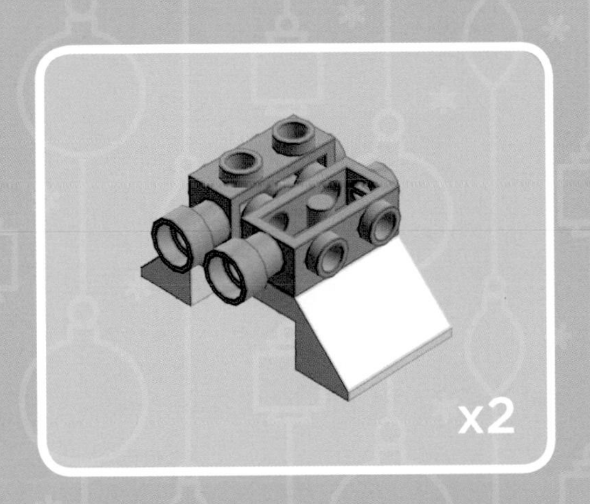
x2

5

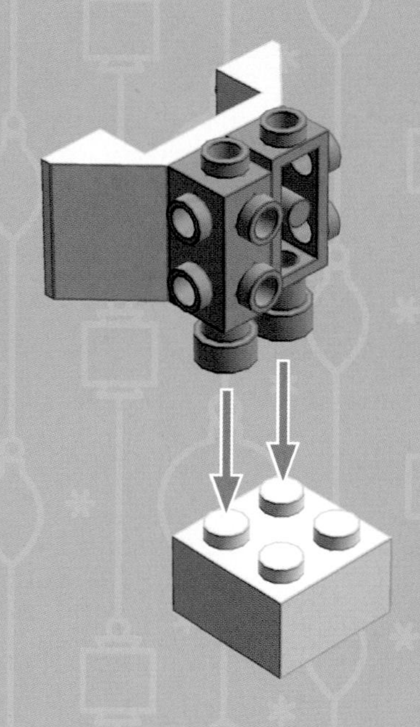

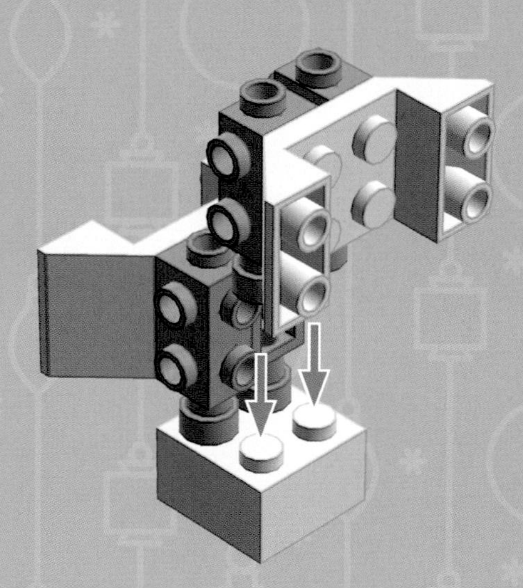

7

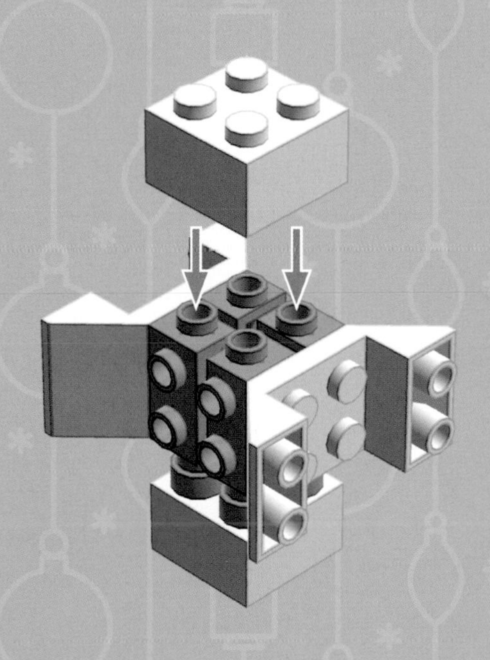

8

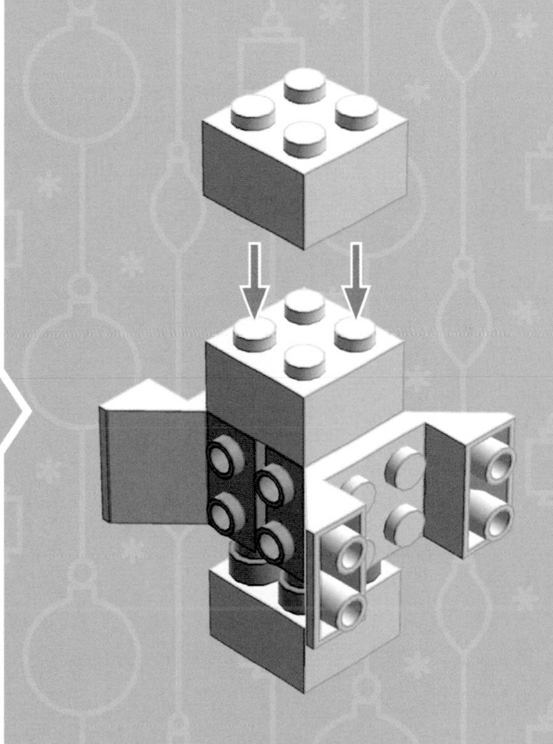

9

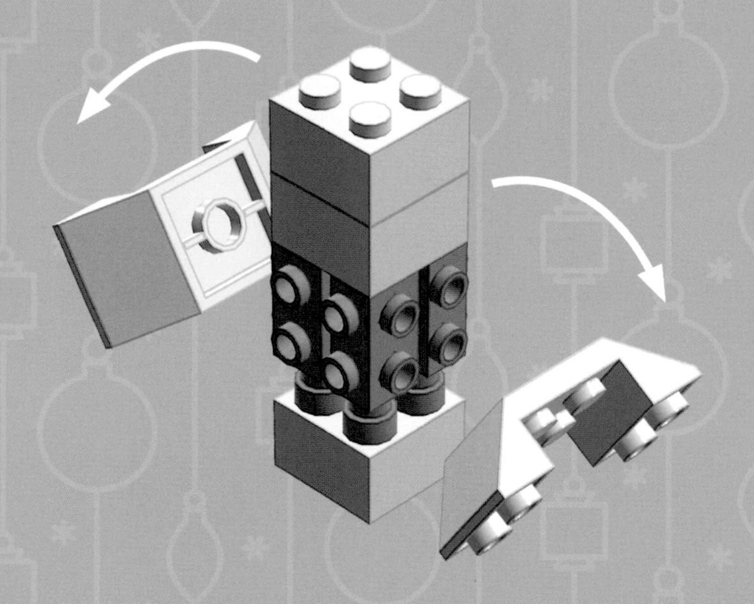

10

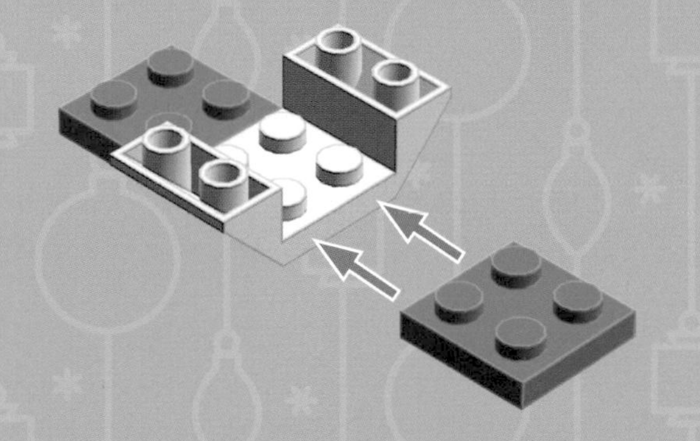

11

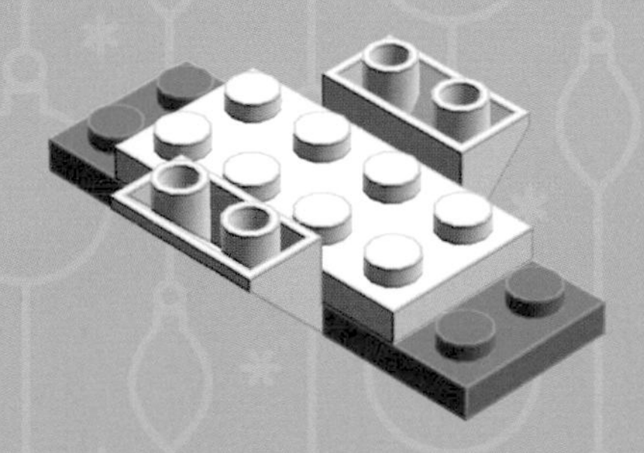

12

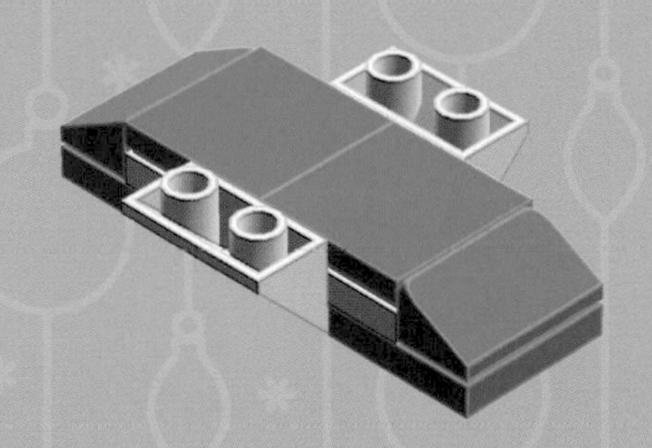

13

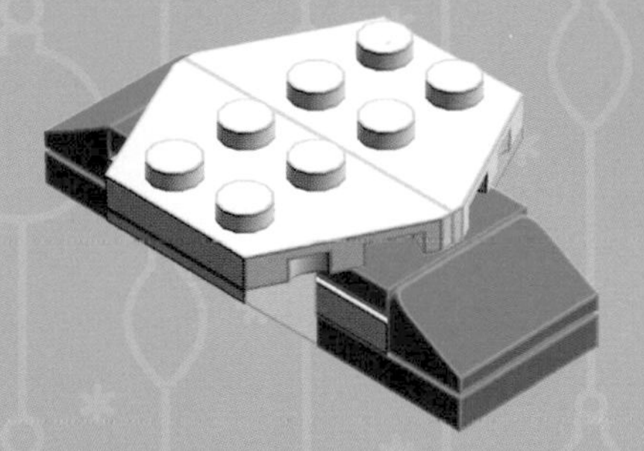

14

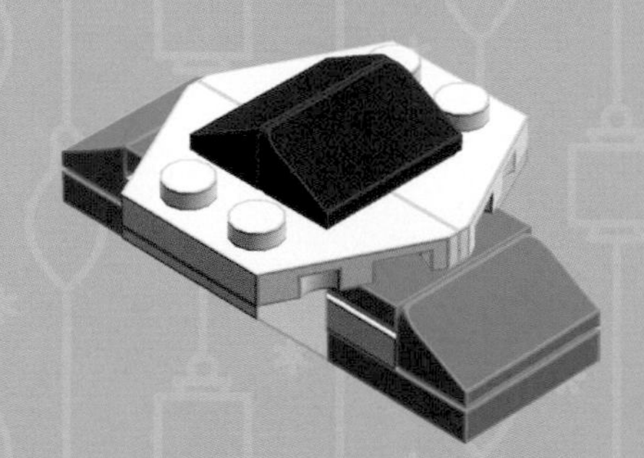

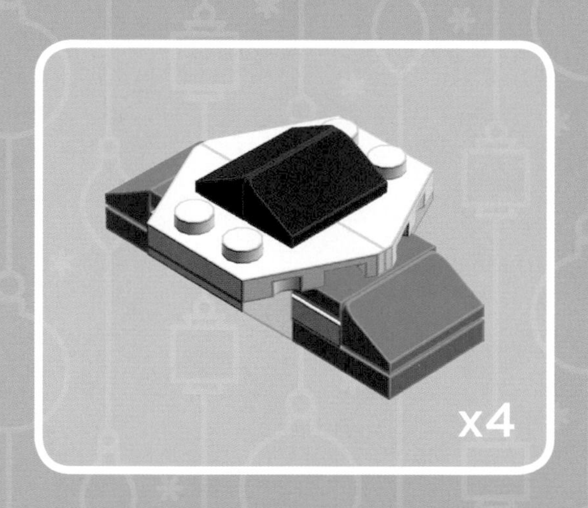

15

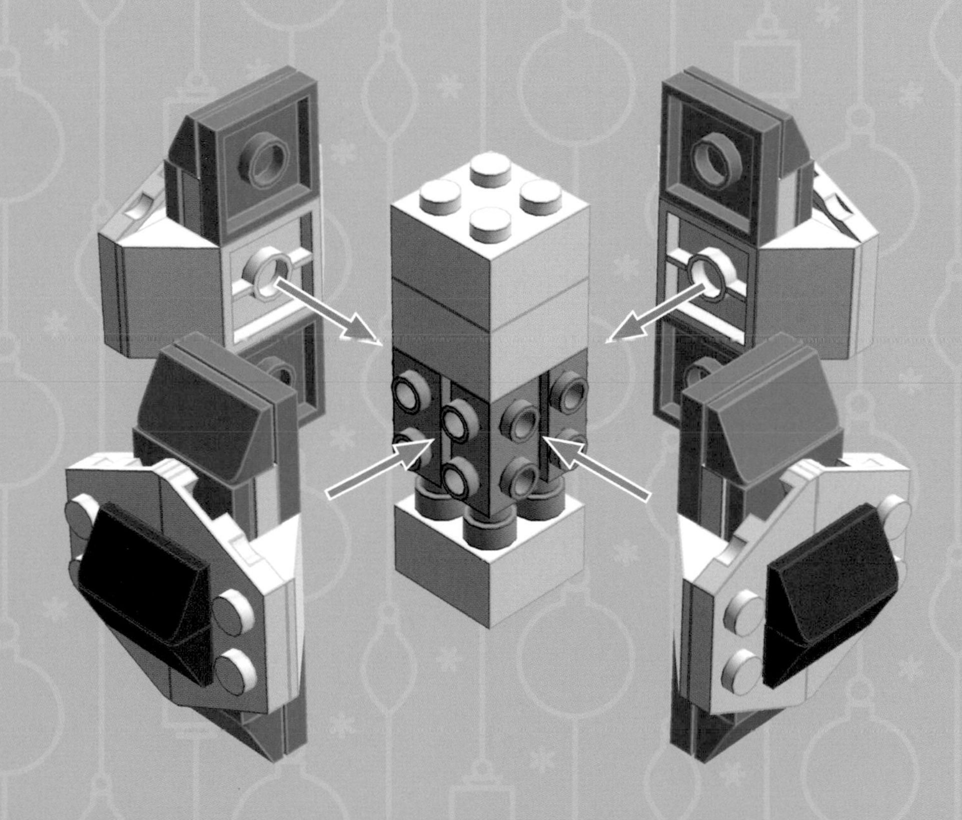

16

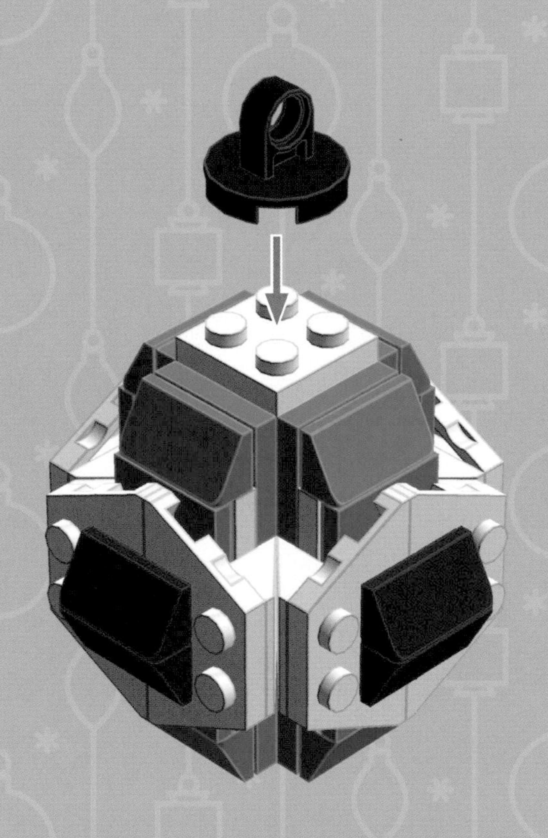

17

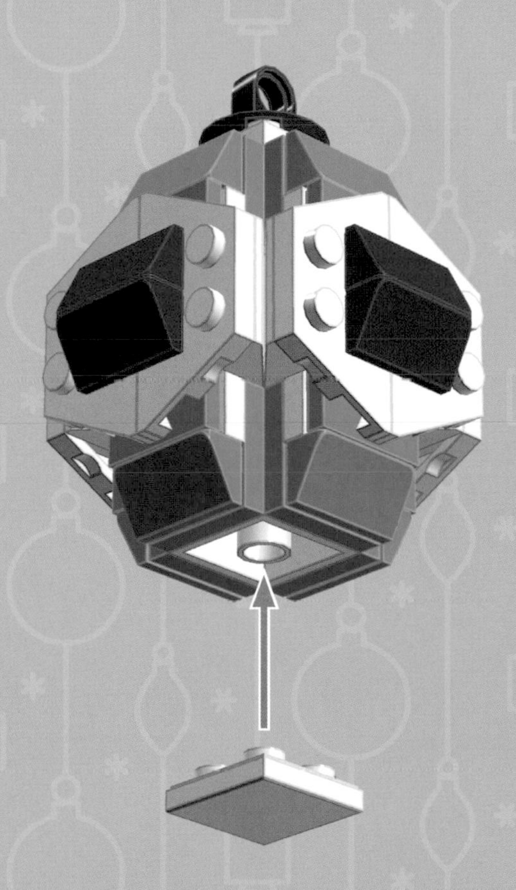

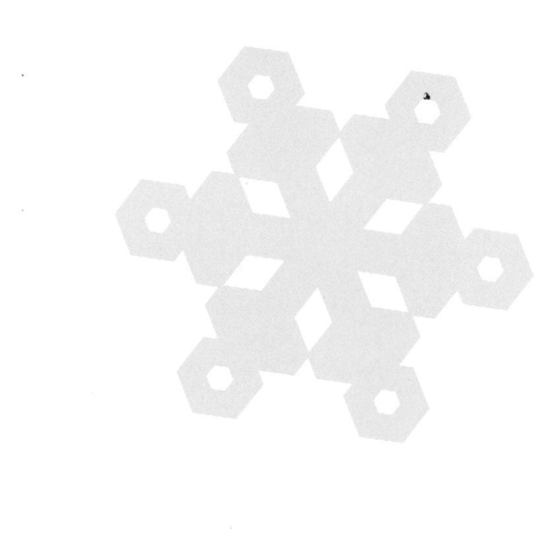

Arcade

4x
614124
2x
6071246
1x
4619636
5x
302326
1x
6039479
3x
306926
2x
362326
2x
243126
1x
4206482
1x
4140801
1x
6030875
1x
281726
1x
6061032
1x
4233487
2x
302121
1x
4180533
1x
4180504
1x
6019217
2x
6066119
2x
366621

1

2

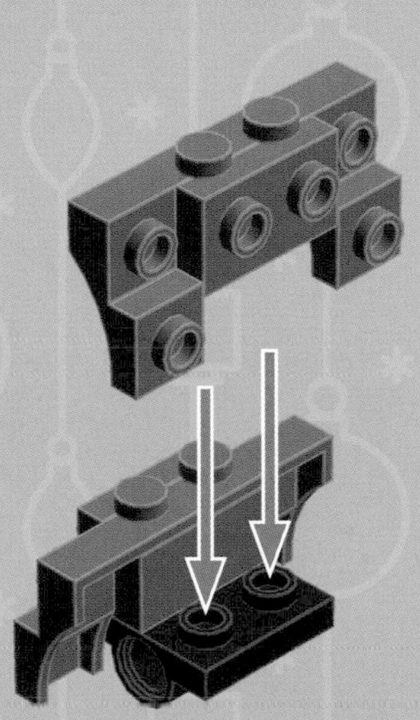

3

4

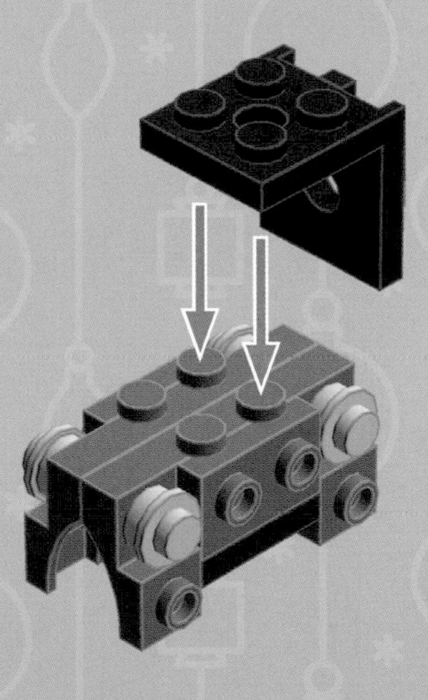

5

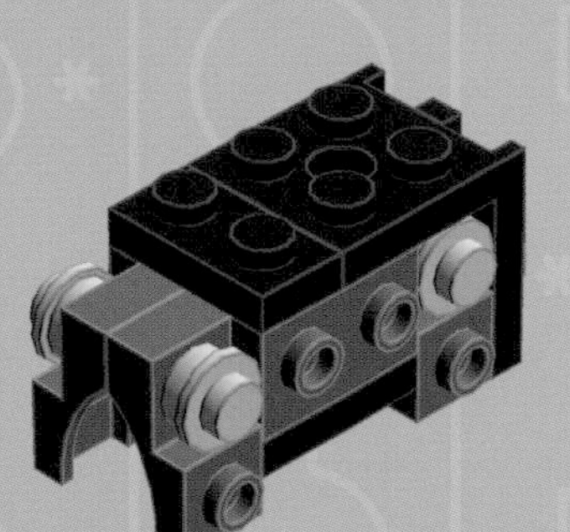

6

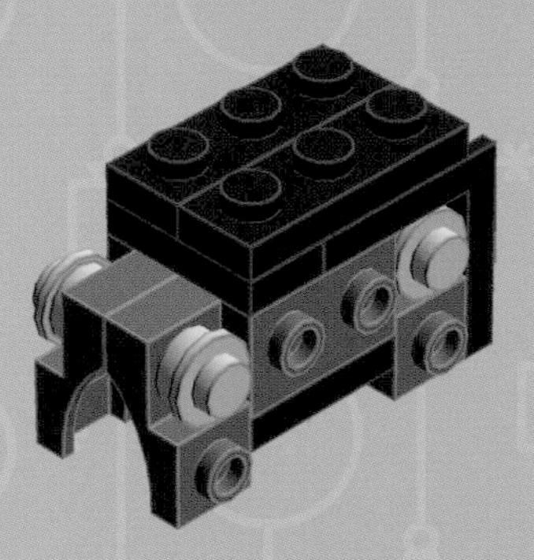

7

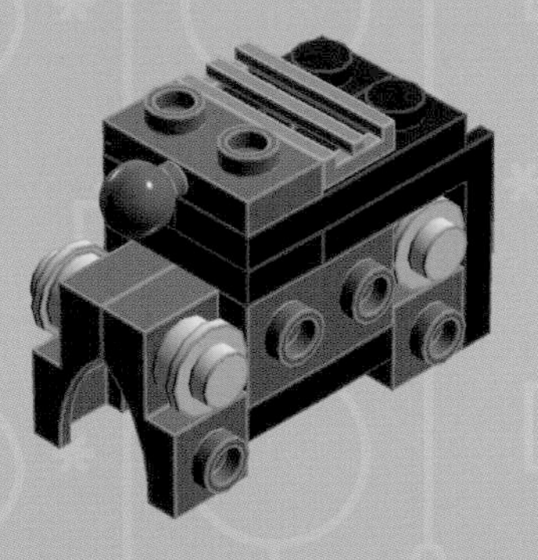

8

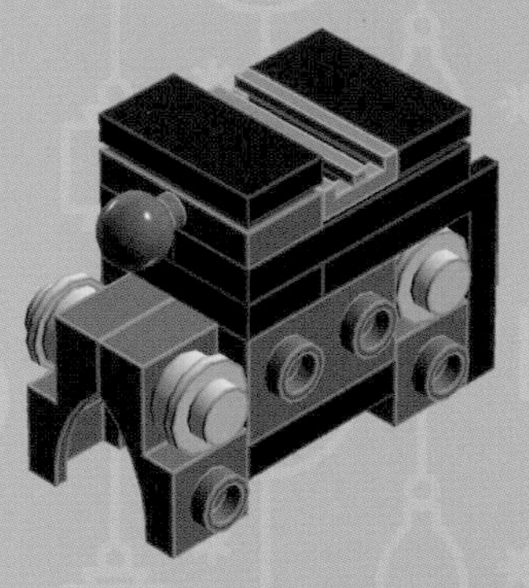

9

10

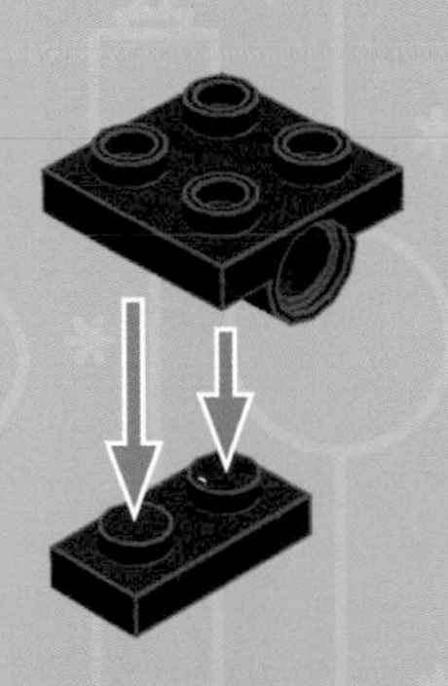

11

12

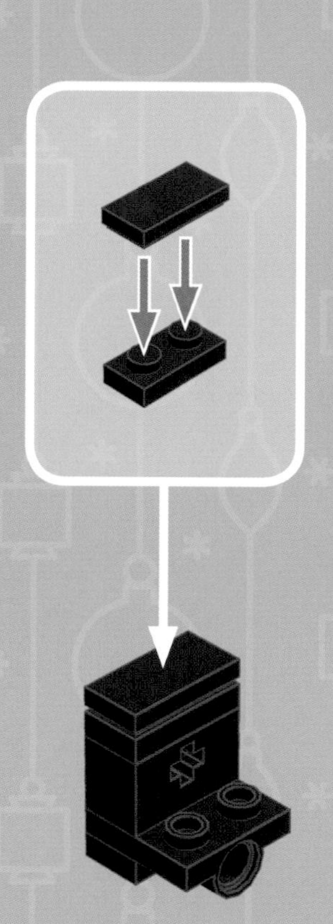

13

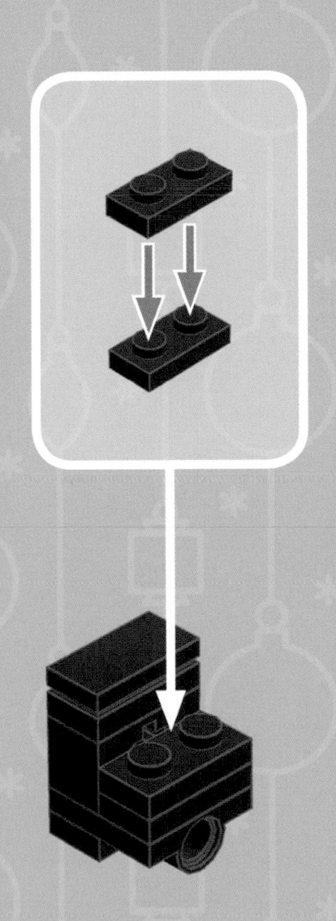

14

15

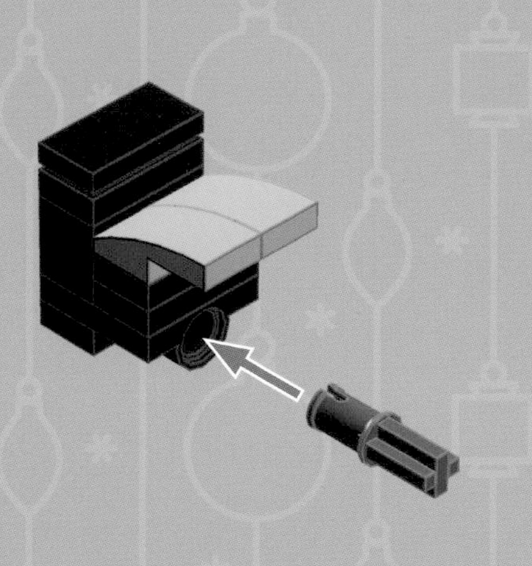

16

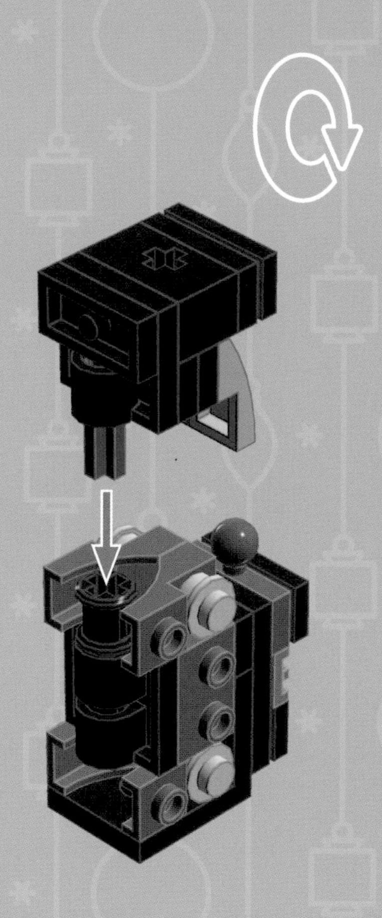

17

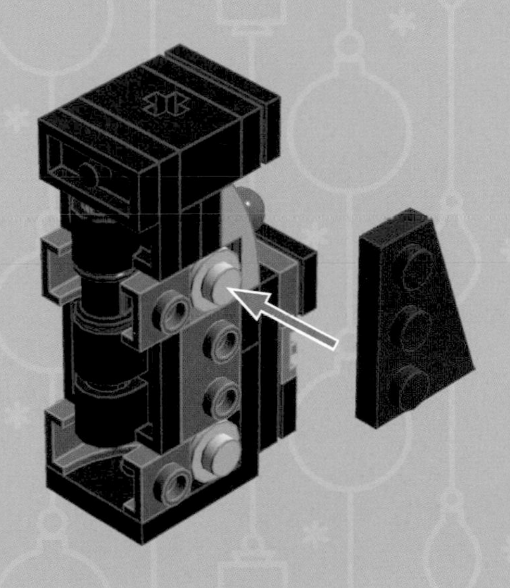

18

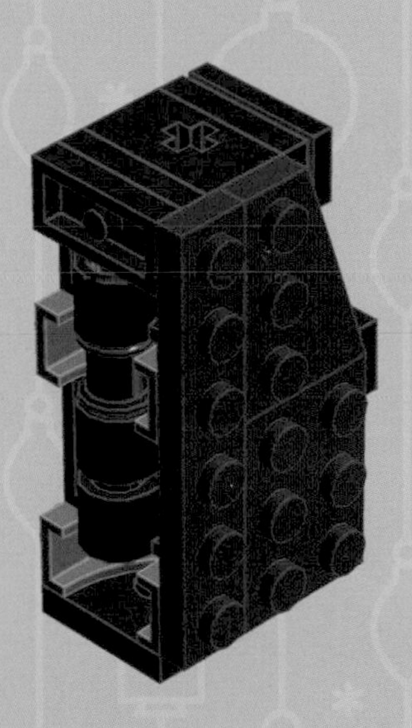

19

20

21

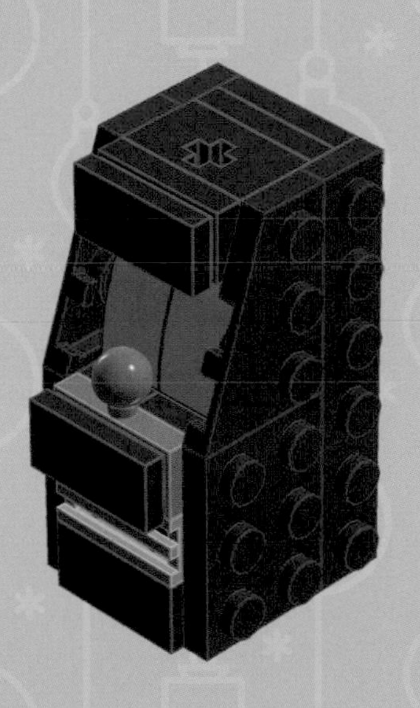

22

23

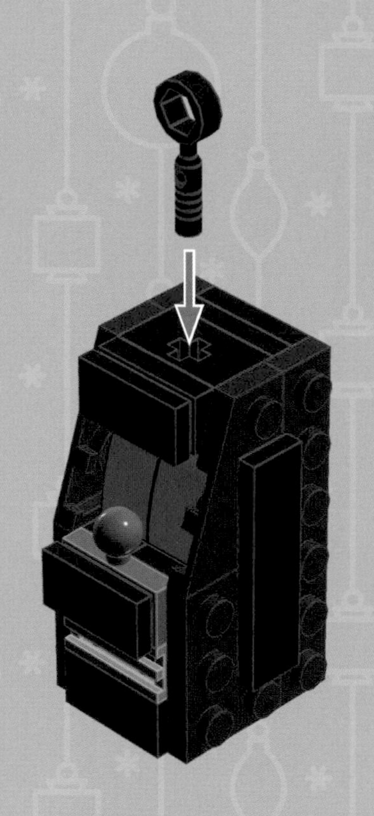

Computer

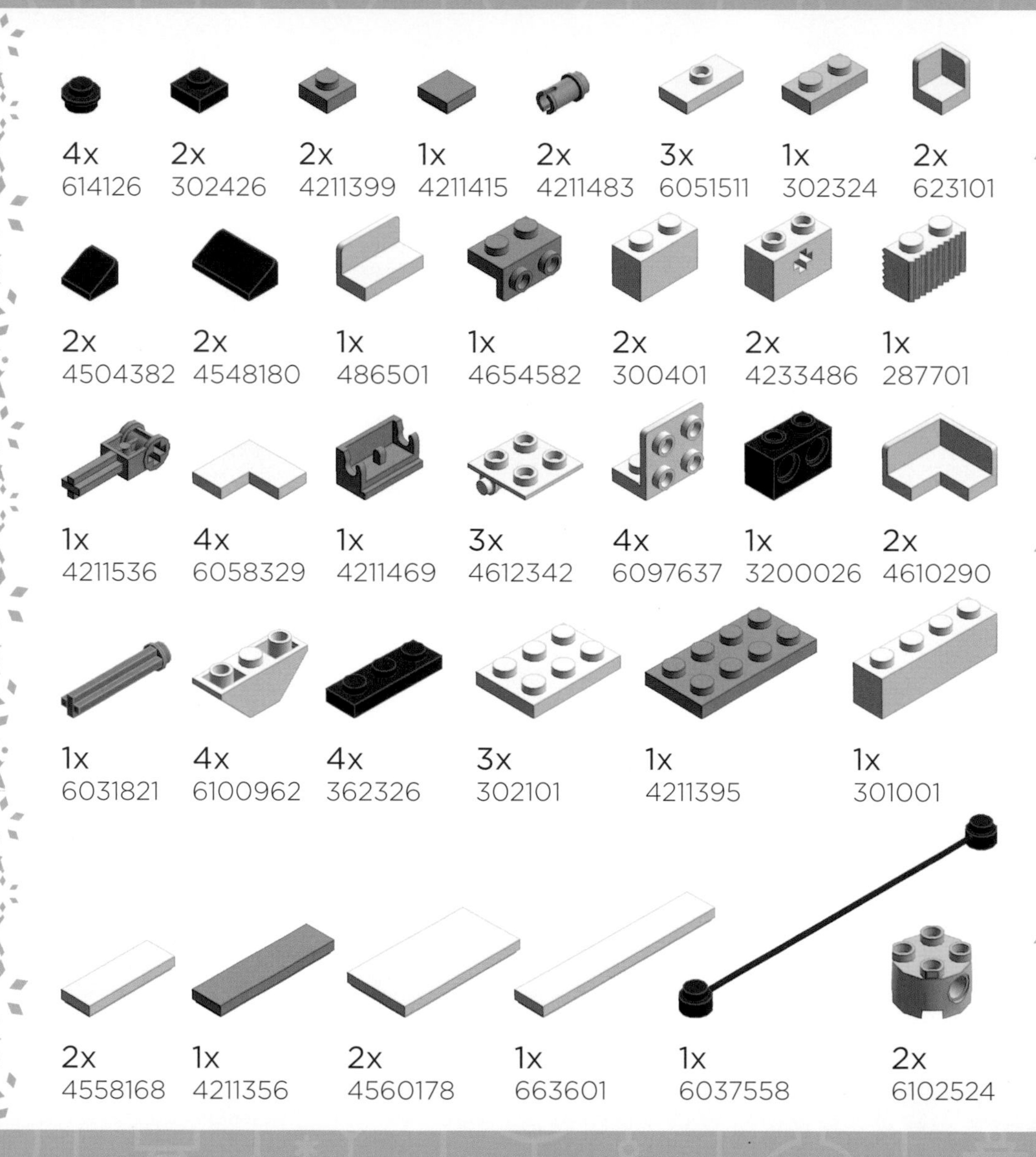
4x 614126
2x 302426
2x 4211399
1x 4211415
2x 4211483
3x 6051511
1x 302324
2x 623101
2x 4504382
2x 4548180
1x 486501
1x 4654582
2x 300401
2x 4233486
1x 287701
1x 4211536
4x 6058329
1x 4211469
3x 4612342
4x 6097637
1x 3200026
2x 4610290
1x 6031821
4x 6100962
4x 362326
3x 302101
1x 4211395
1x 301001
2x 4558168
1x 4211356
2x 4560178
1x 663601
1x 6037558
2x 6102524

1

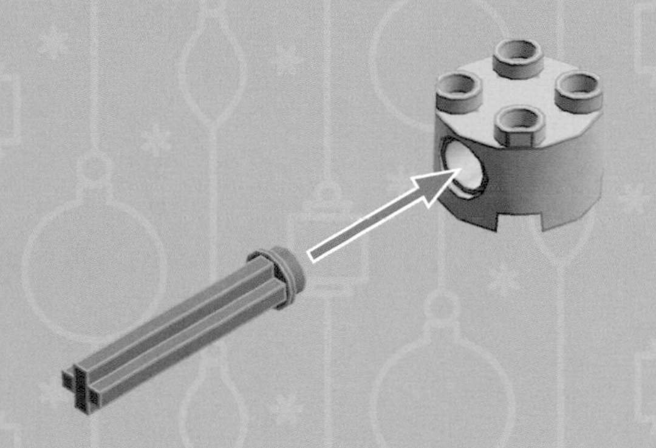

2

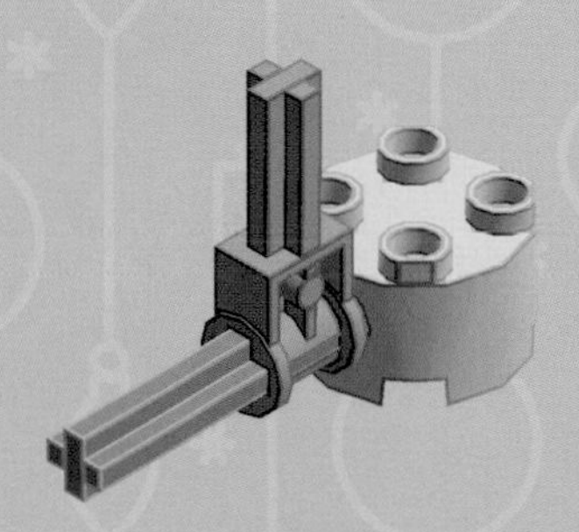

3

4

5

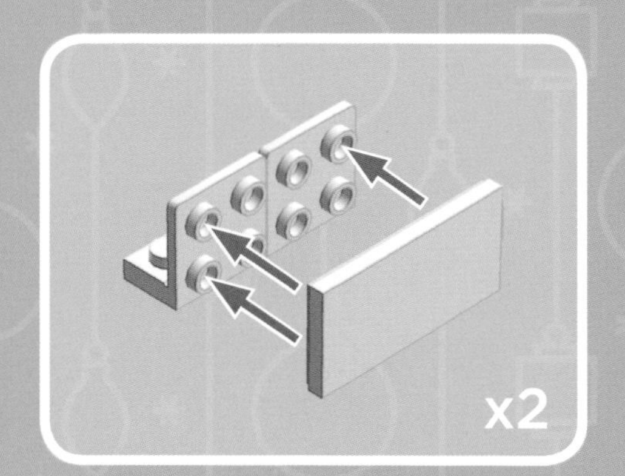

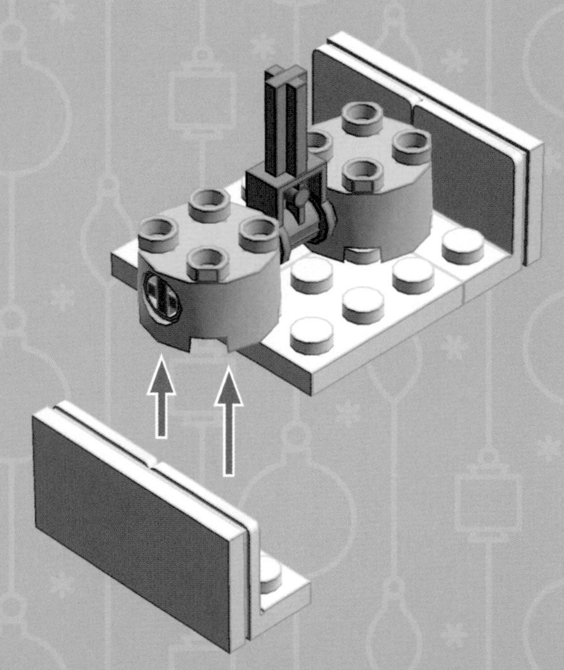

6

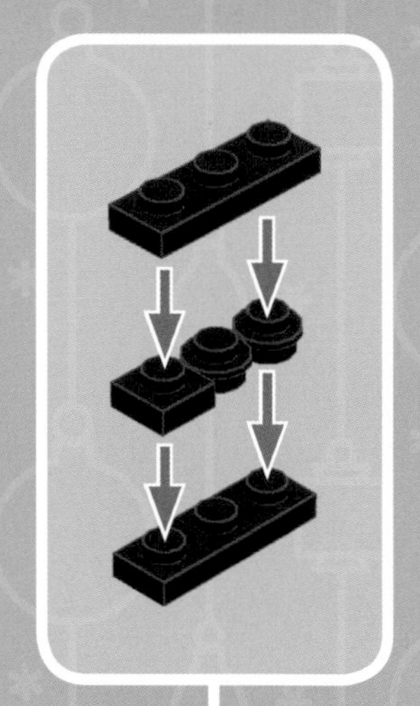

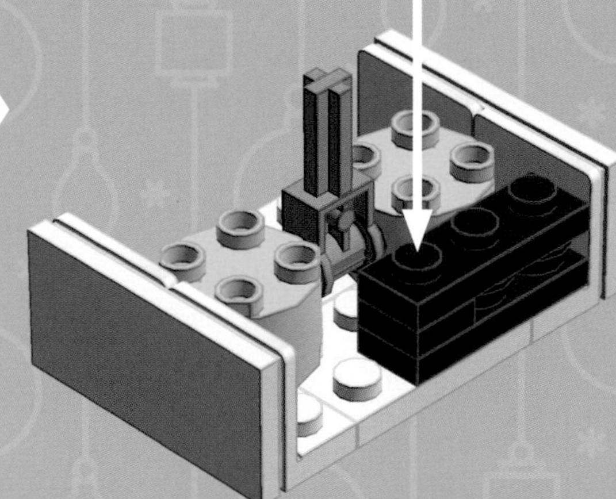

7

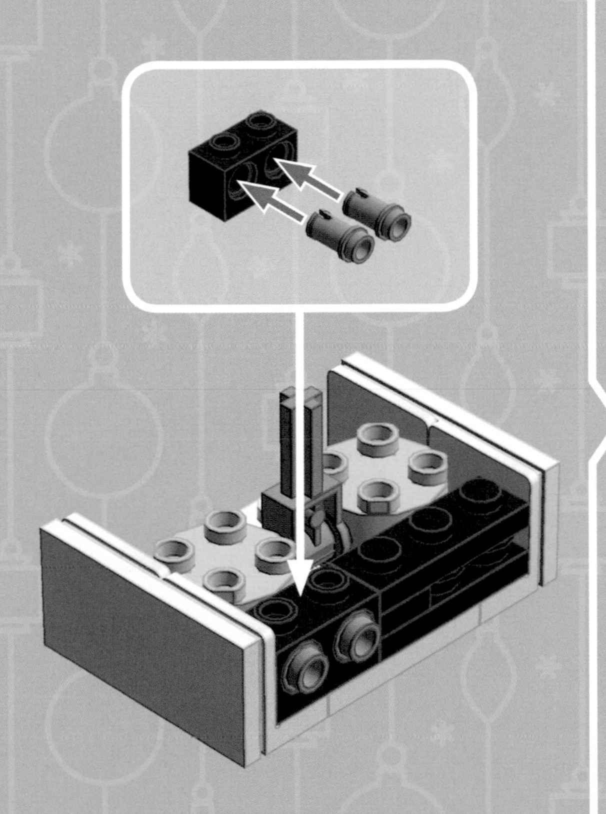

8

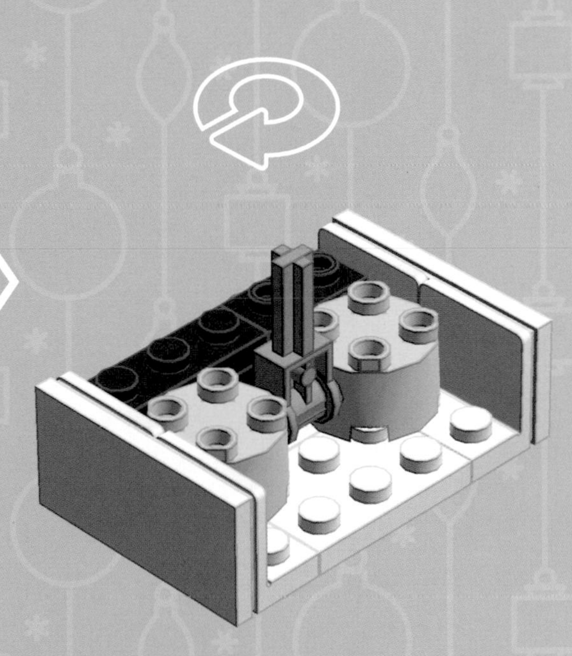

9

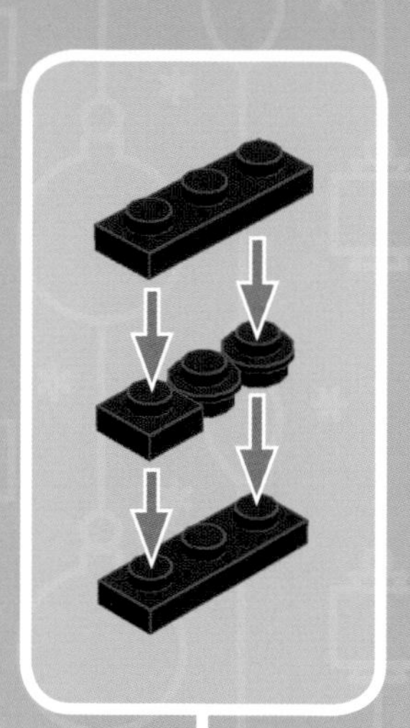

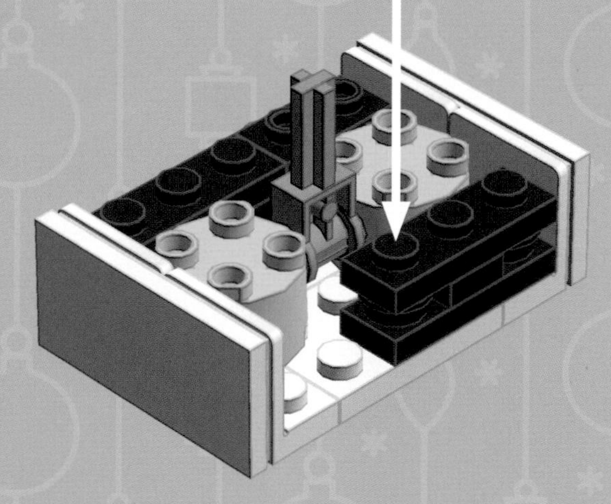

10

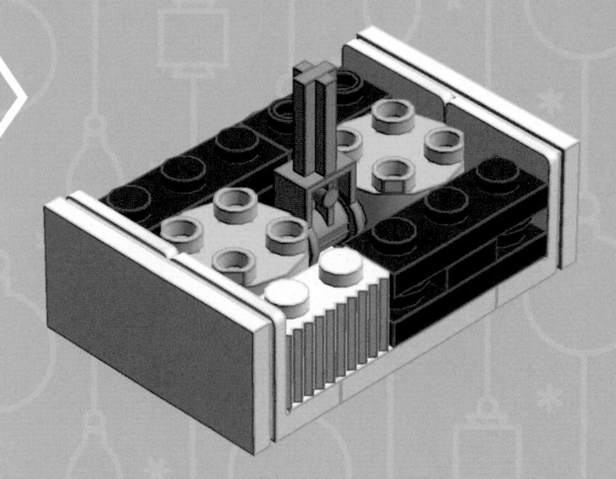

11

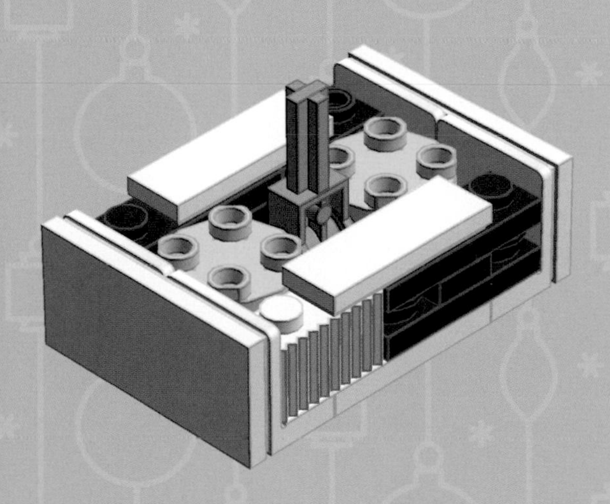

12

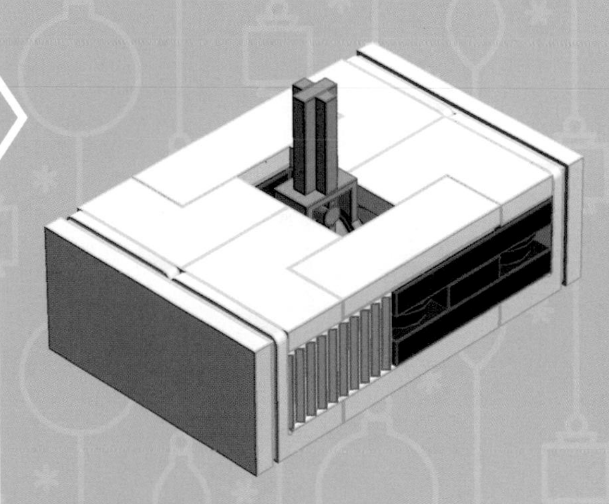

13

14

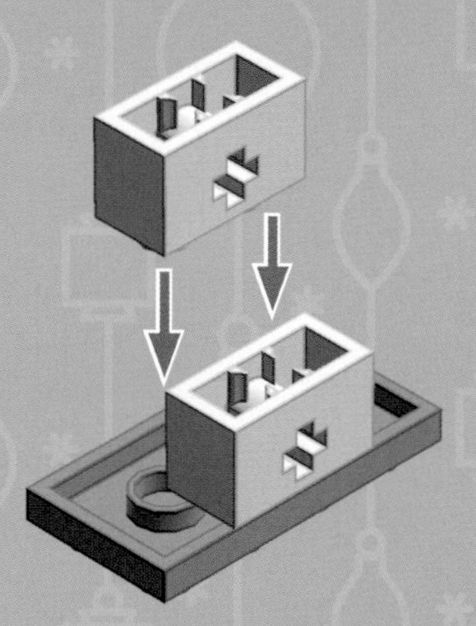

15

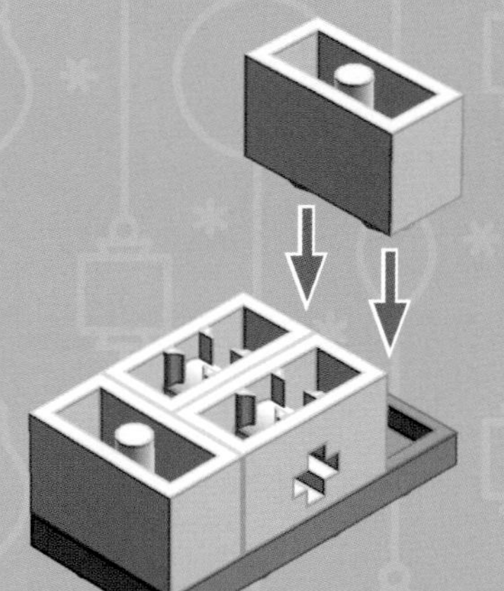

16

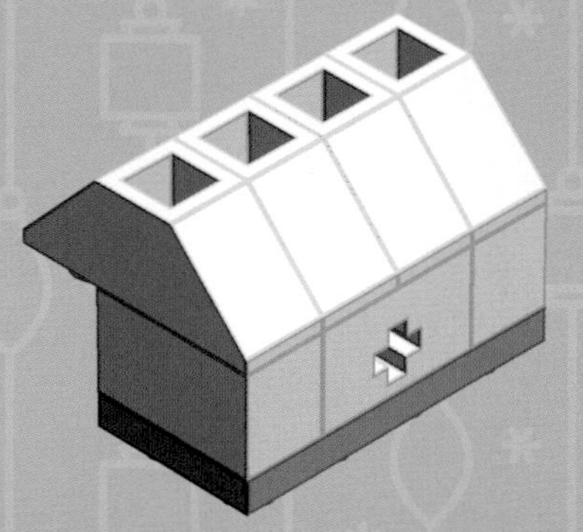

17

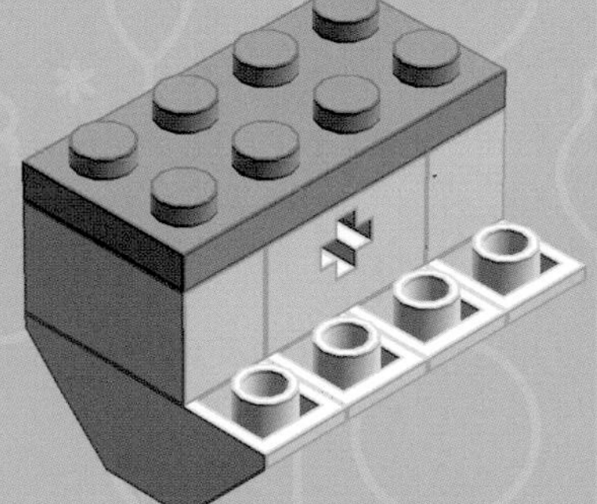

18

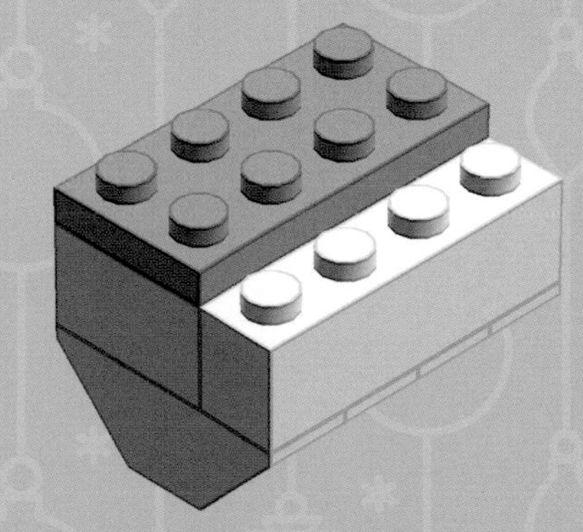

19

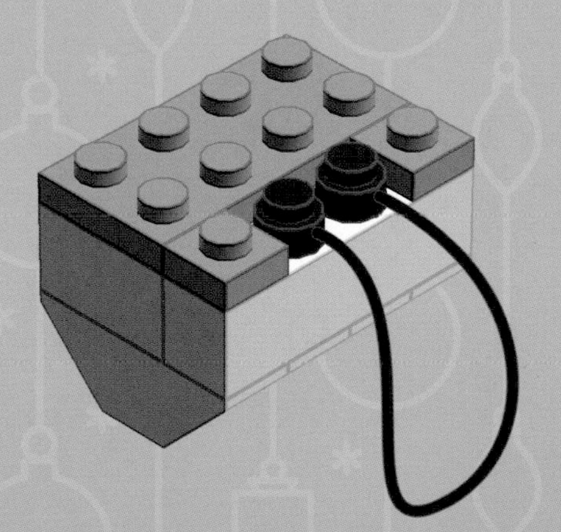

20

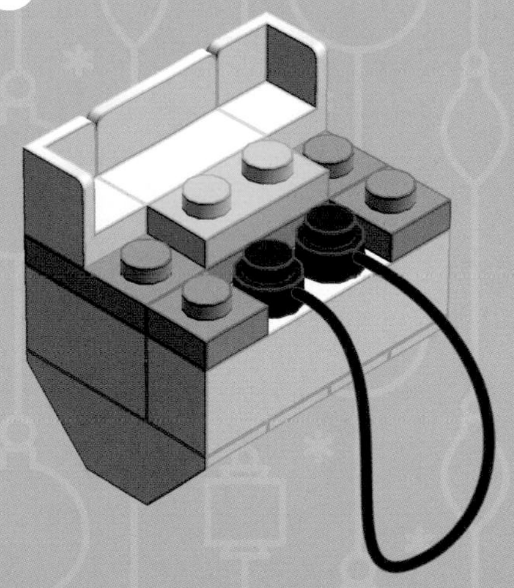

21

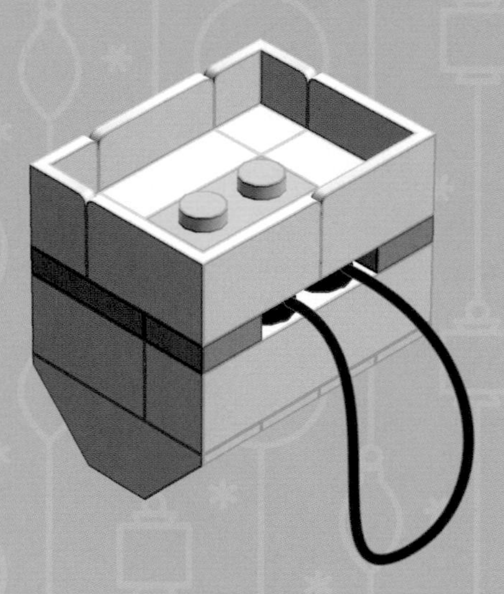

22

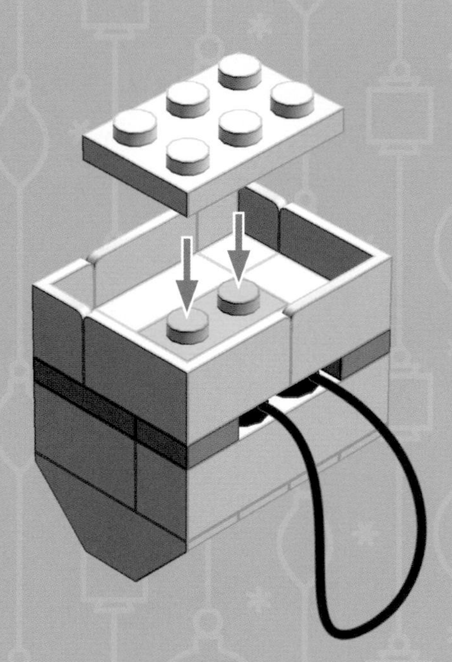

23

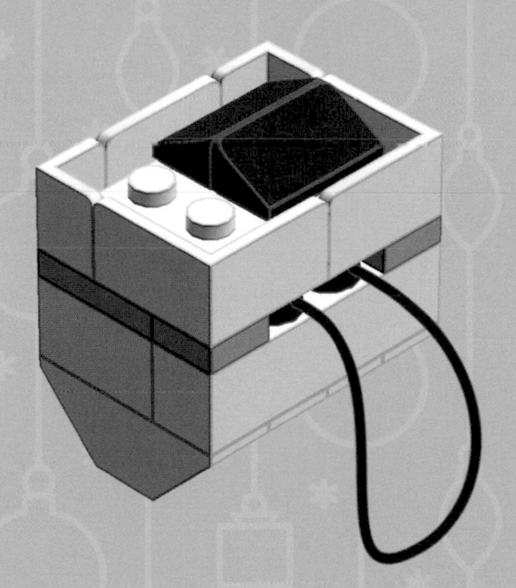

24

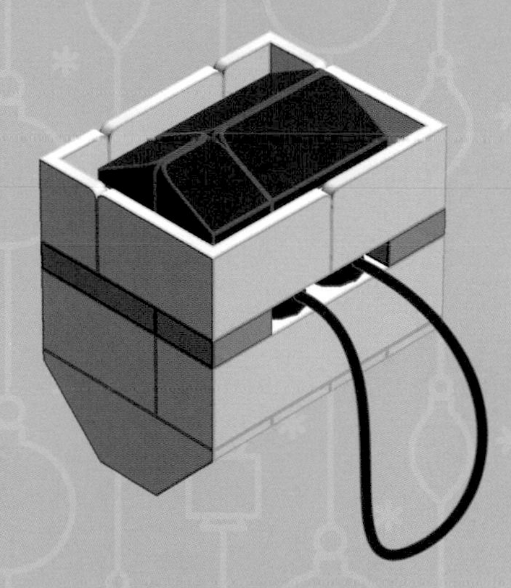

25

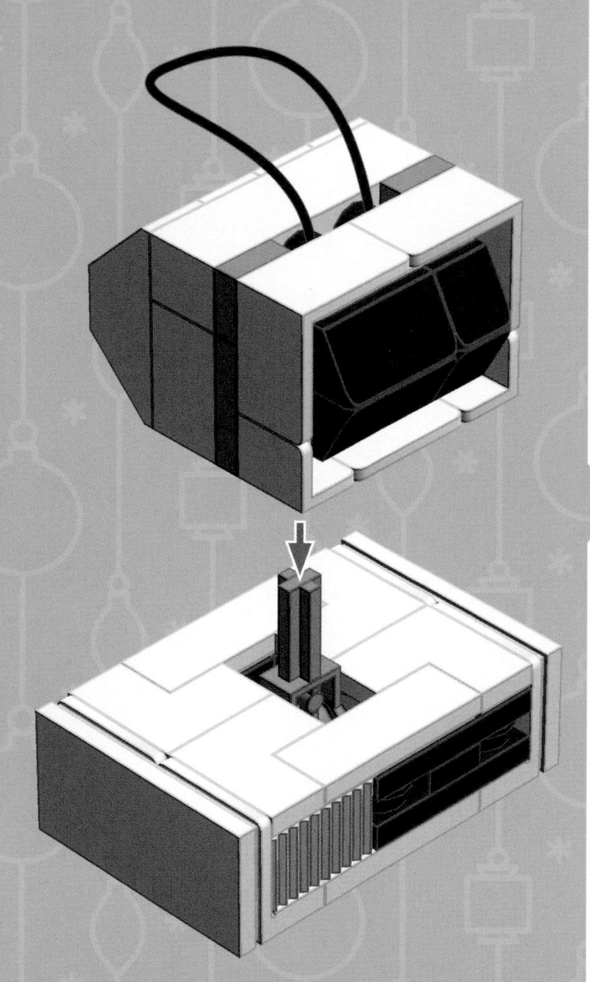

26

27

28

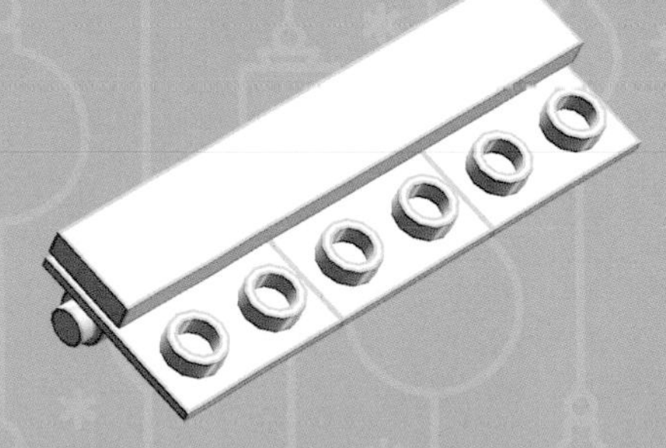

29

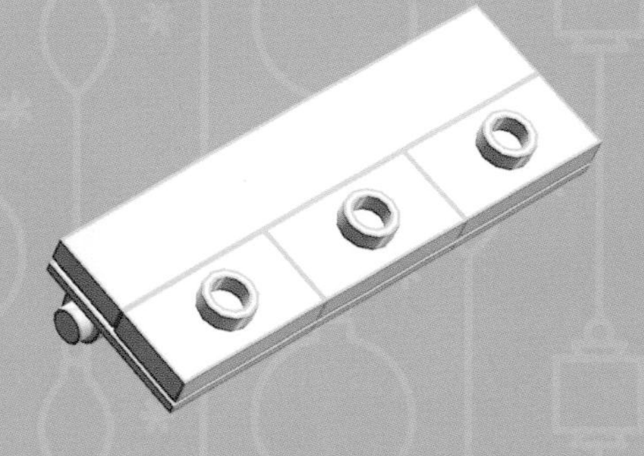

30

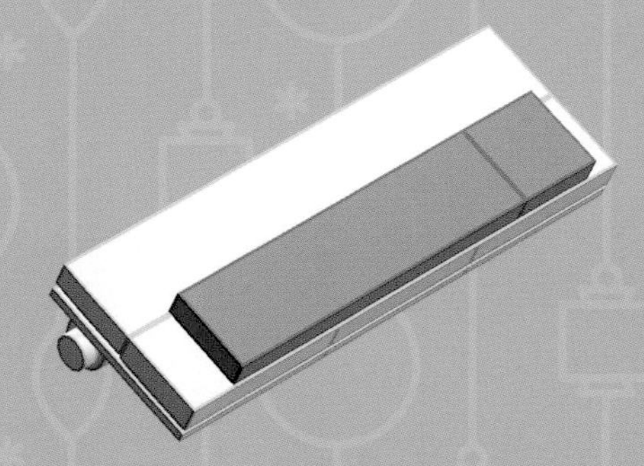

31

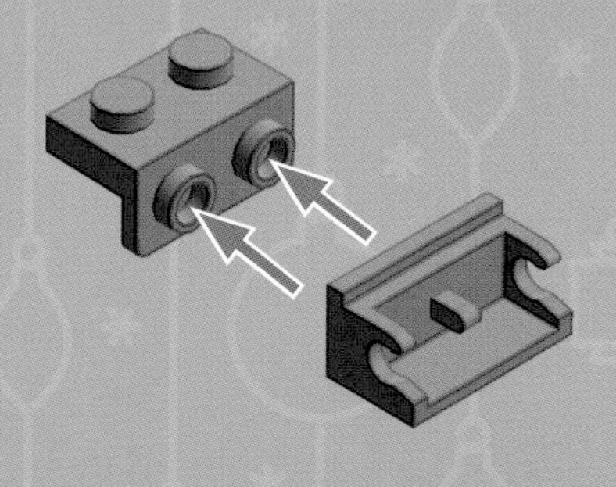

32

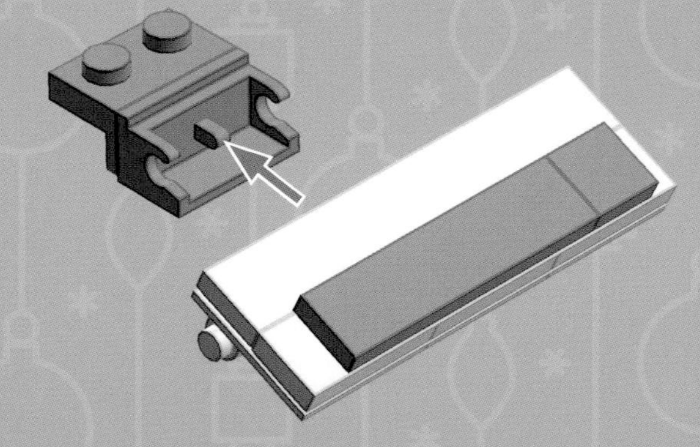

33

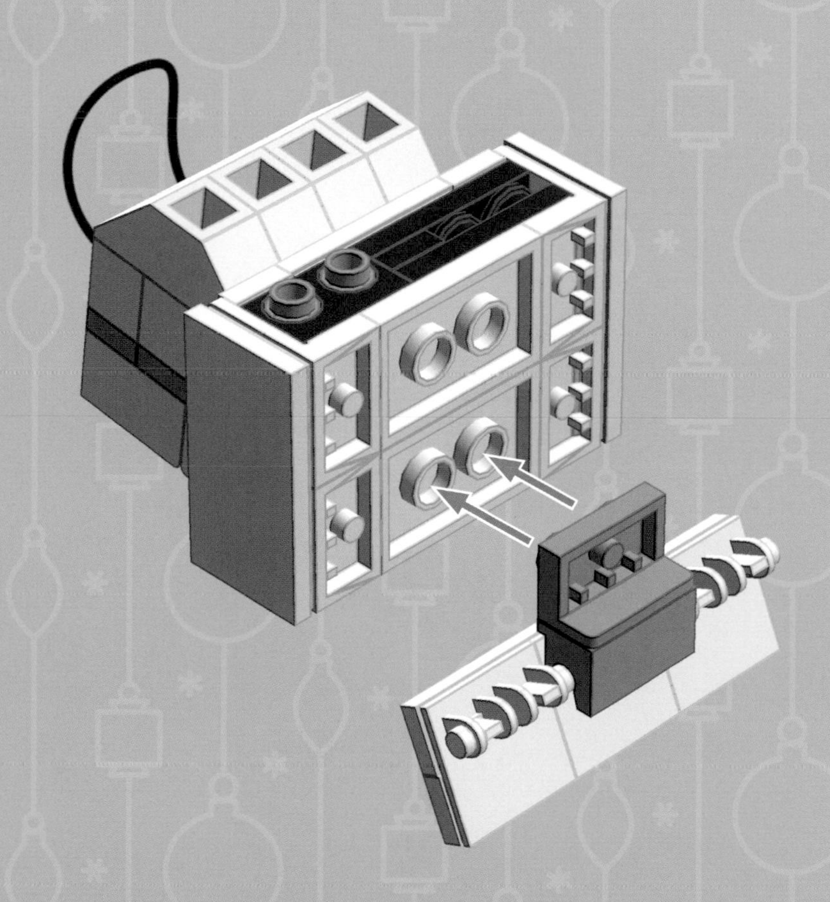

34

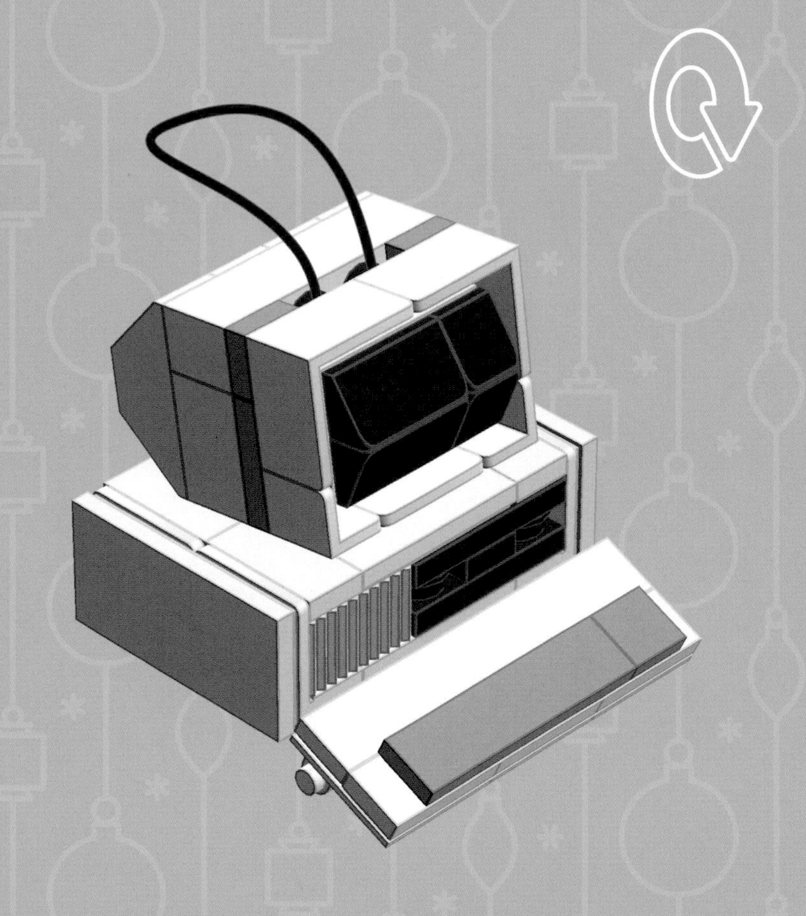

Camera

1x
4655241

1x
4646844

2x
307001

1x
6047501

1x
4210719

4x
6099728

4x
6034044

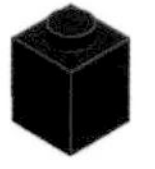
2x
300526

2x
4558954

2x
4541191

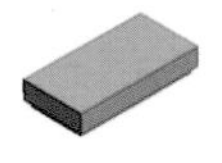
6x
4622062

4x
6028736

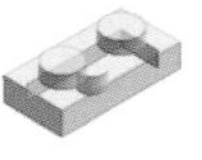
4x
4167842

2x
6092585

4x
6099730

1x
6093053

1x
306826

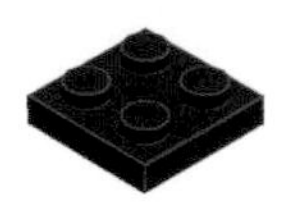
1x
302226

4x
6000650

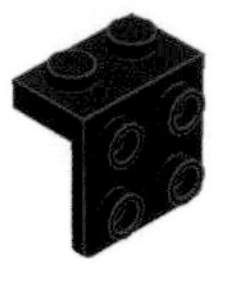
4x
6117973

4x
4211056
2x
4211100
2x
4211542
1x
4299389
1x
4186513
1x
302126
2x
6133826
1x
4533412
2x
371026
2x
6072668
1x
243101
1x
4520320

1

2

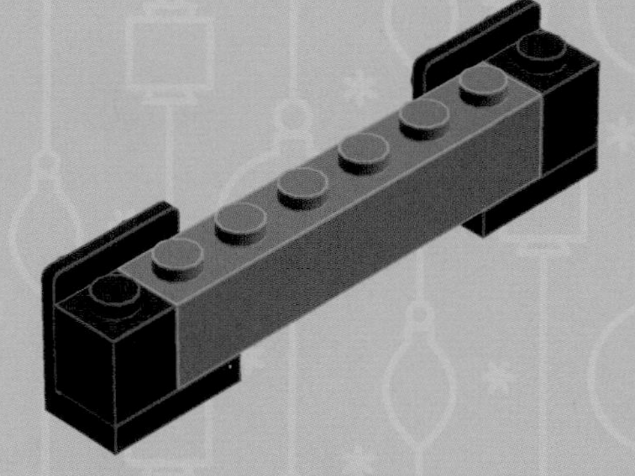

3

4

5

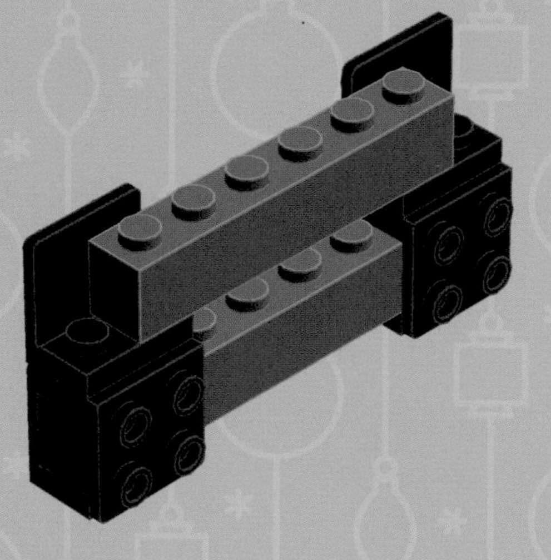

6

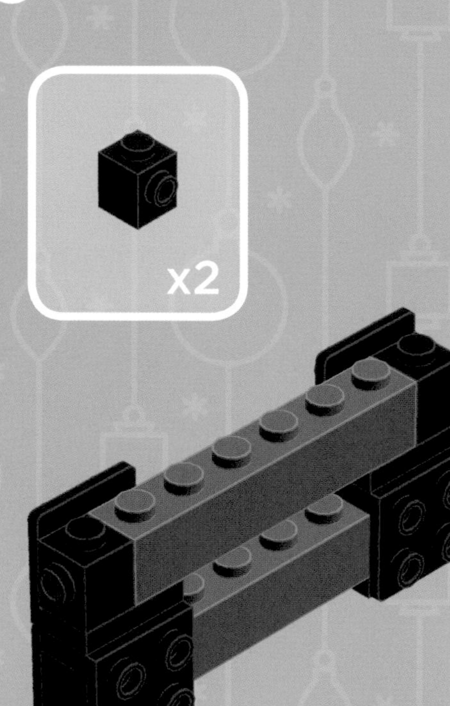

7

8

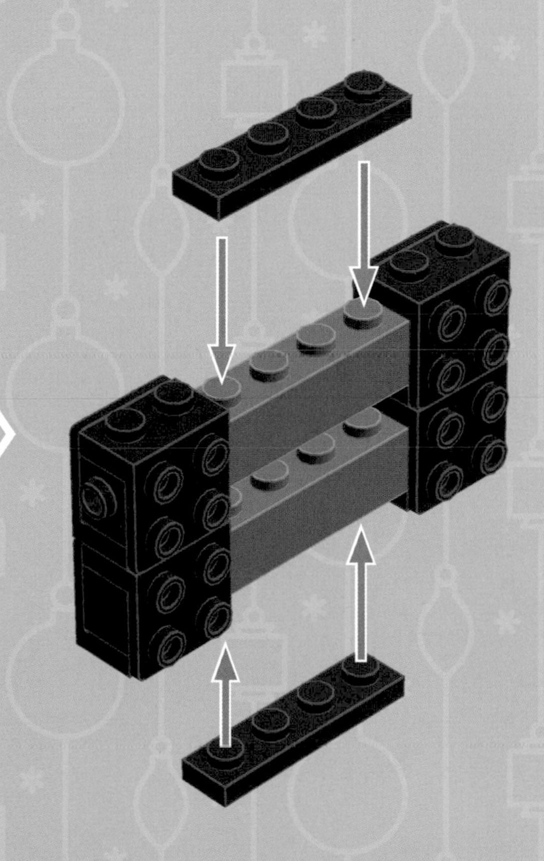

9

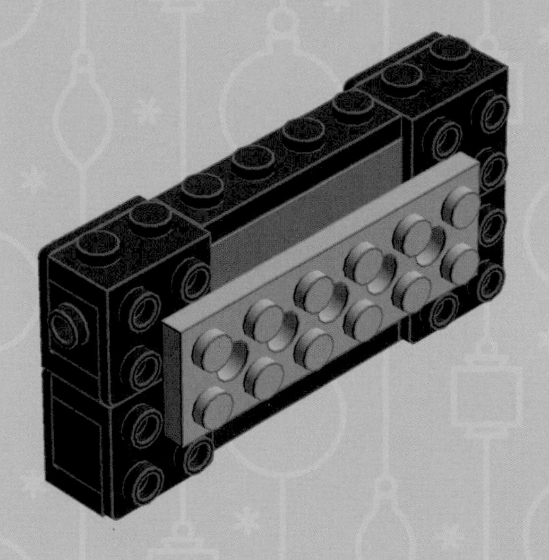

10

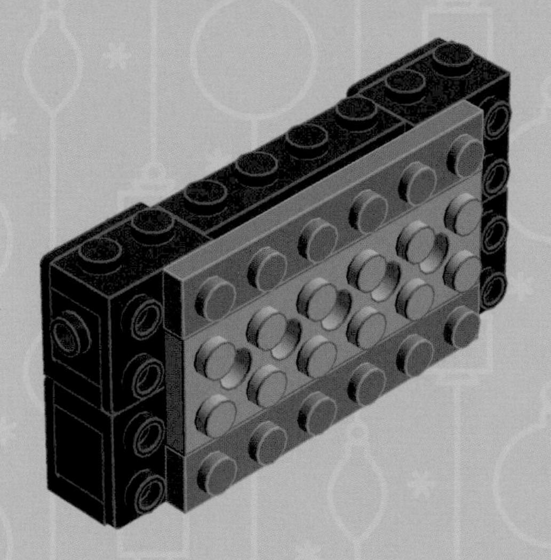

11

12

13

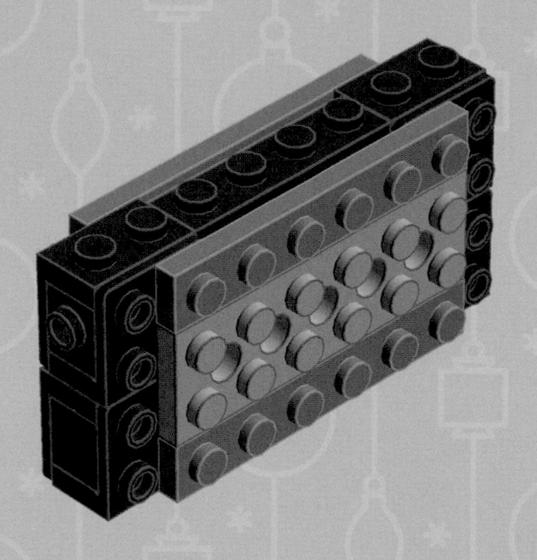

14

15

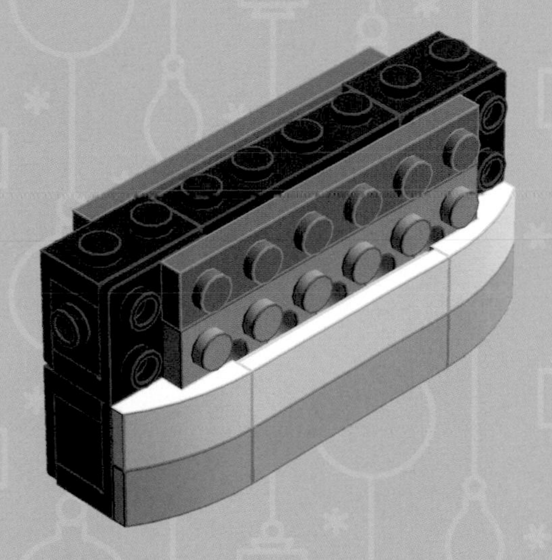

16

17

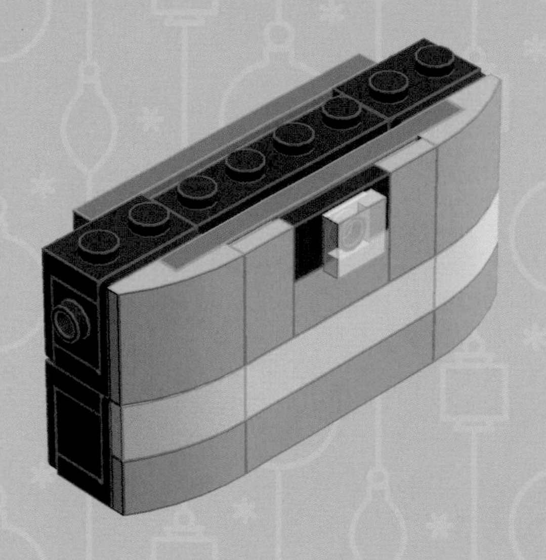

18

19

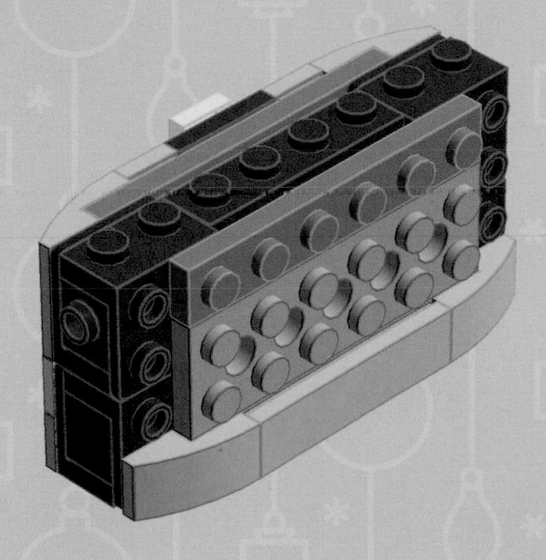

20

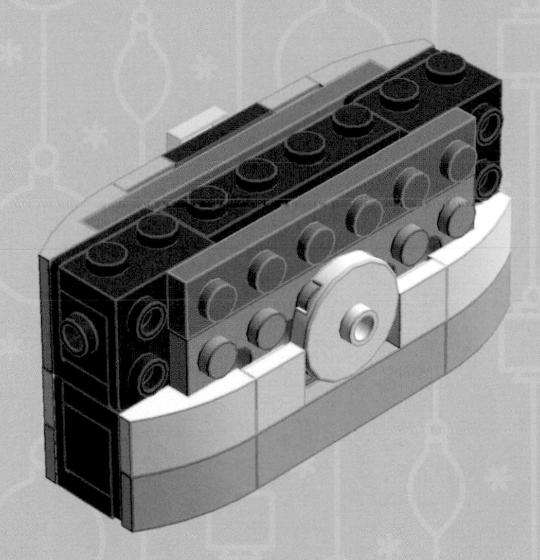

21

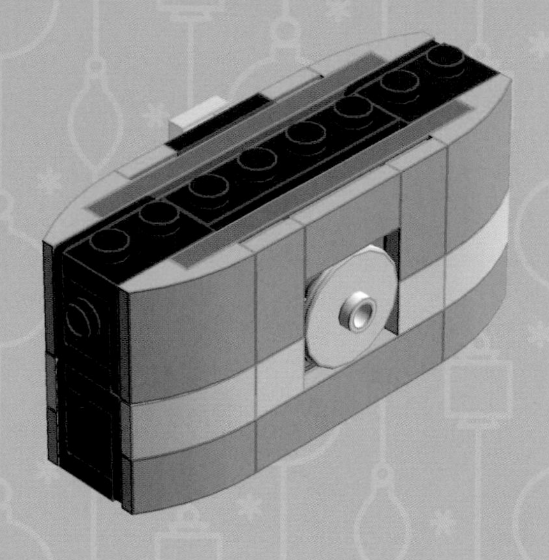

22

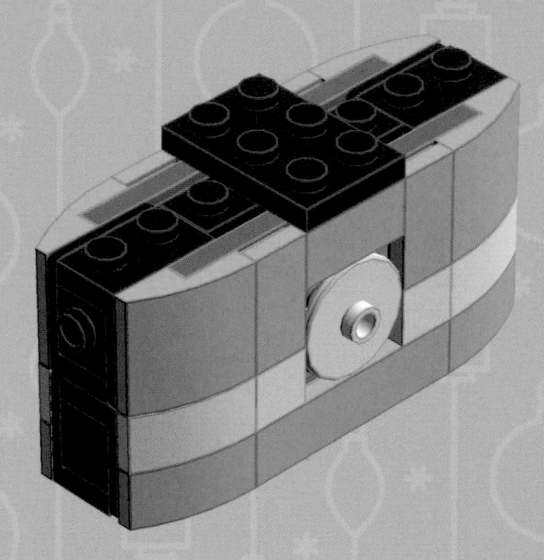

23

24

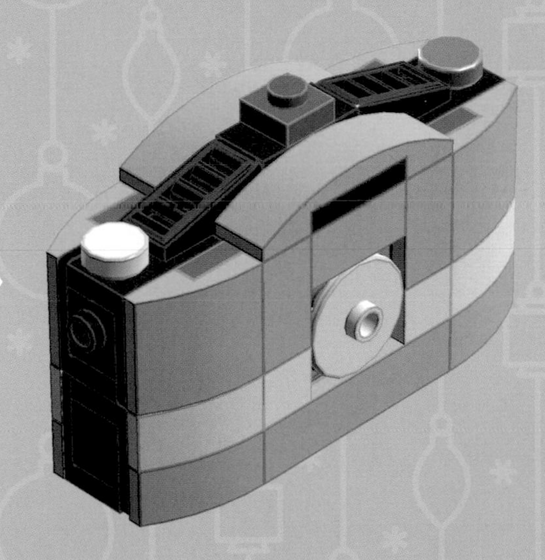

25

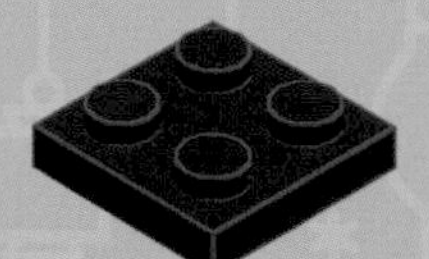

26

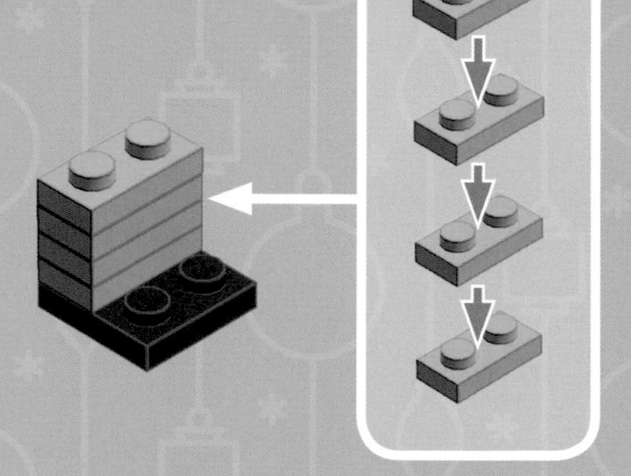

27

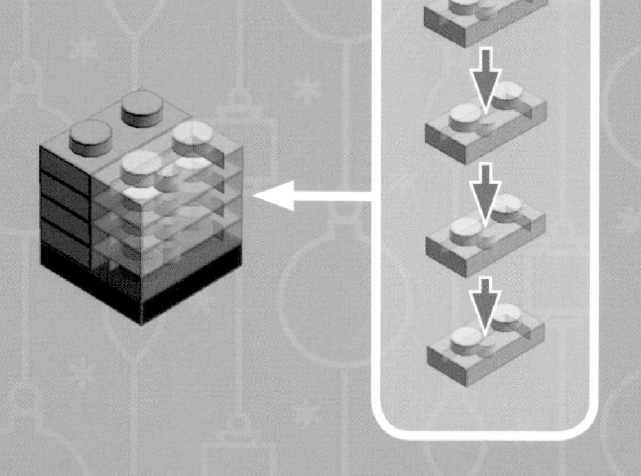

28

29

30

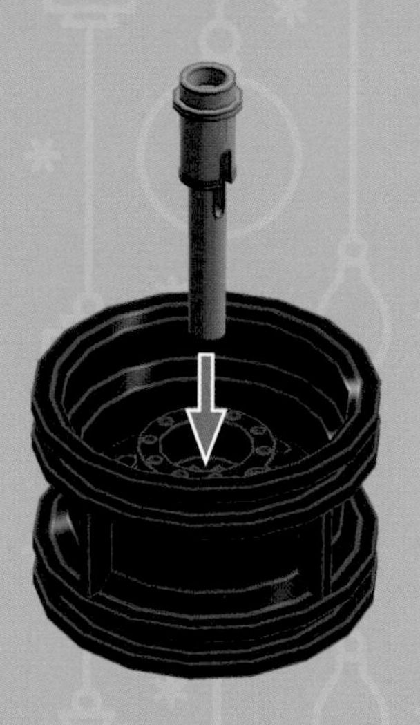

31

32

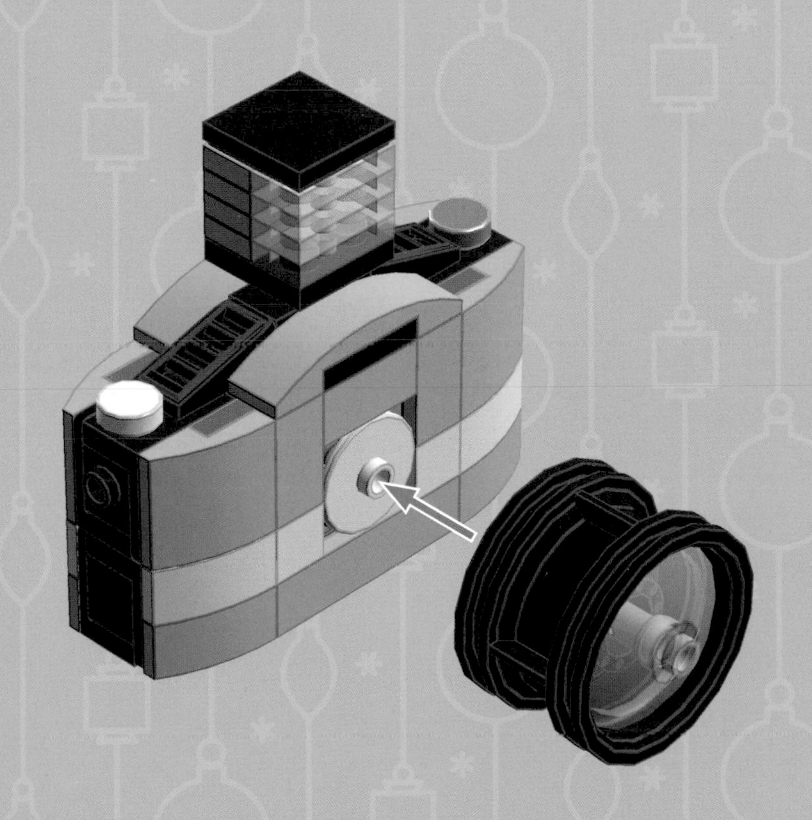

33

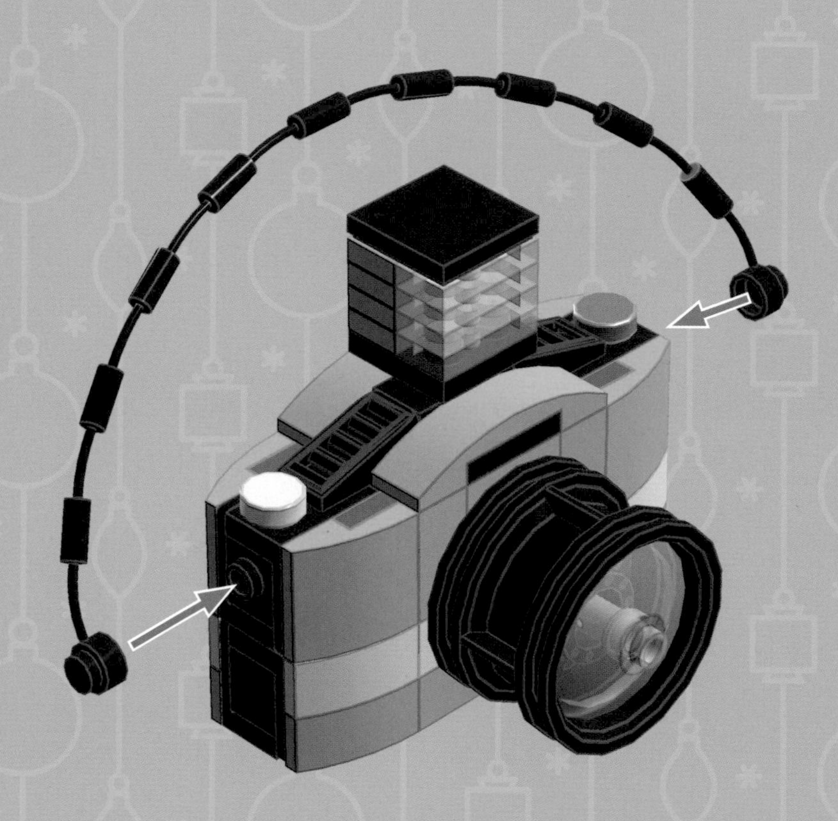

34

Burger

4x
4161734

4x
4211150

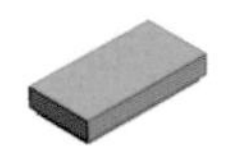

2x
4622062

2x
4297083

8x
4211257

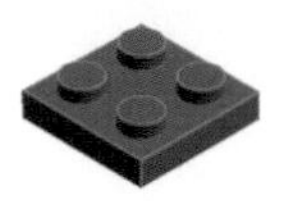

2x
4615606

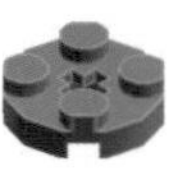

2x
403228

2x
403221

1x
6010831

8x
4159196

1x
4114306

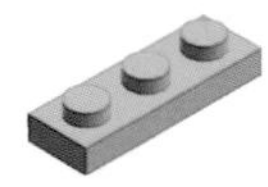

4x
4210210

2x
6020073

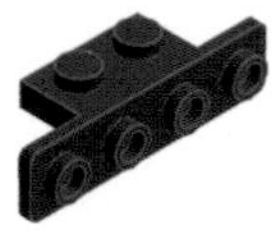

4x
6123759

2x
4211186

4x
4666611

4x
4539908

4x
6020145

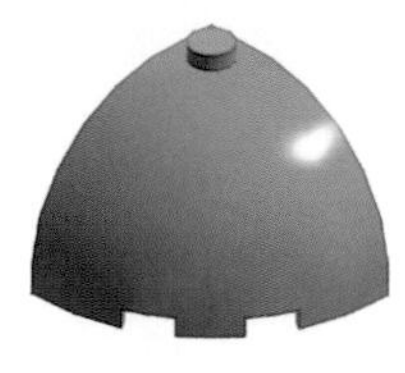

4x
6057435

1

2

3

4

5

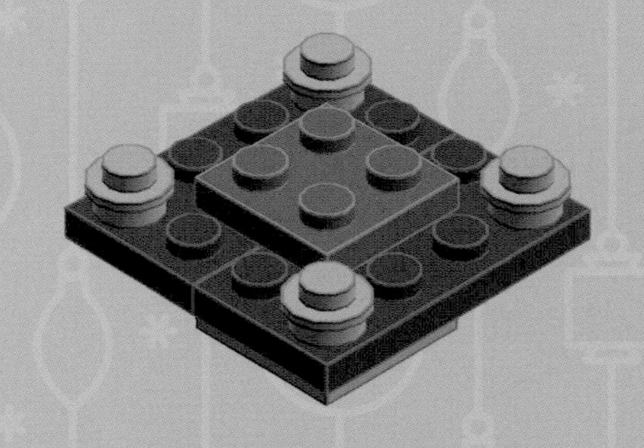

6

7

8

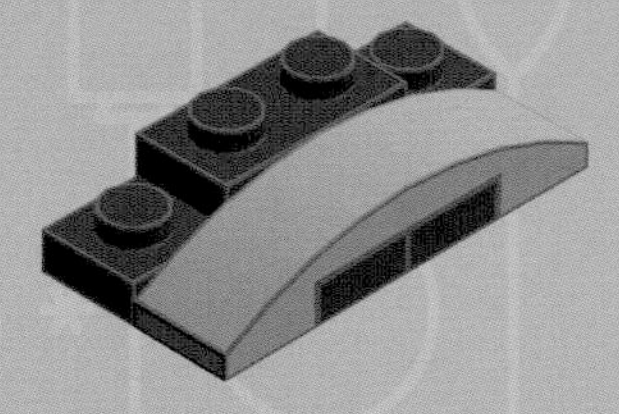

9

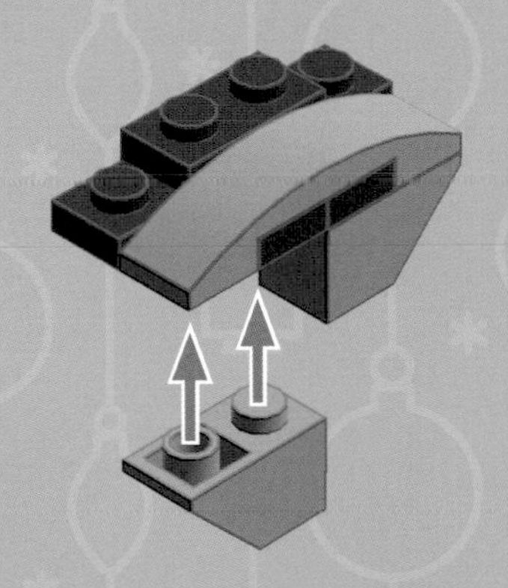

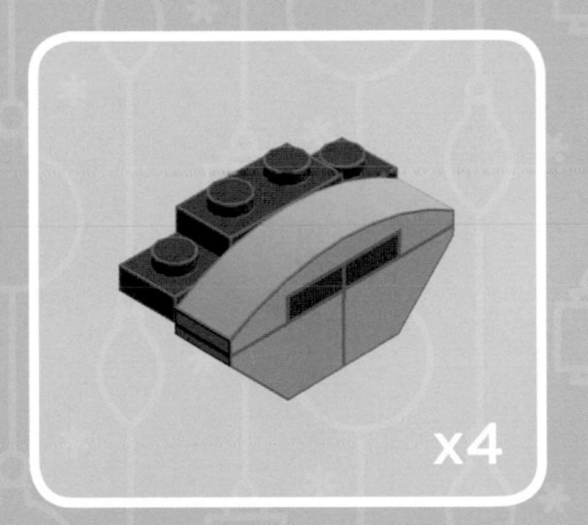

10

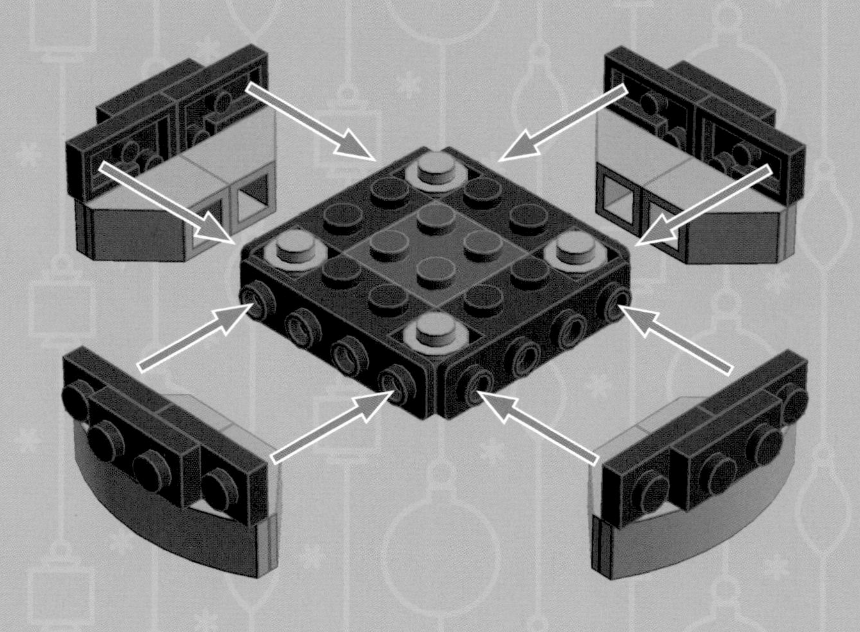

11

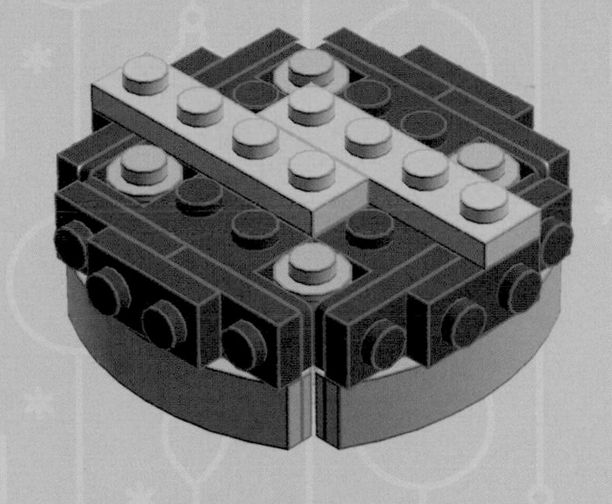

12

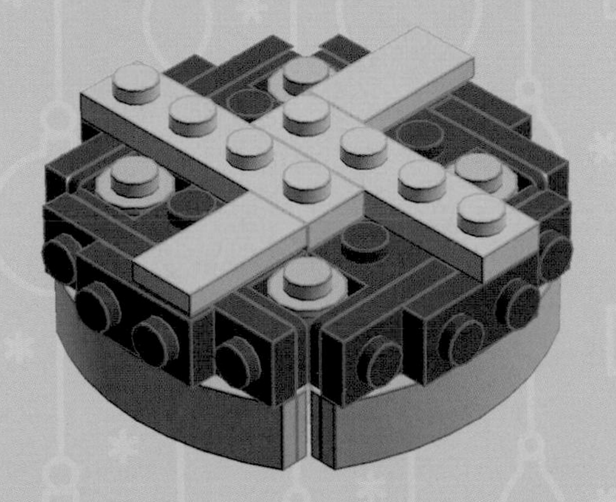

13

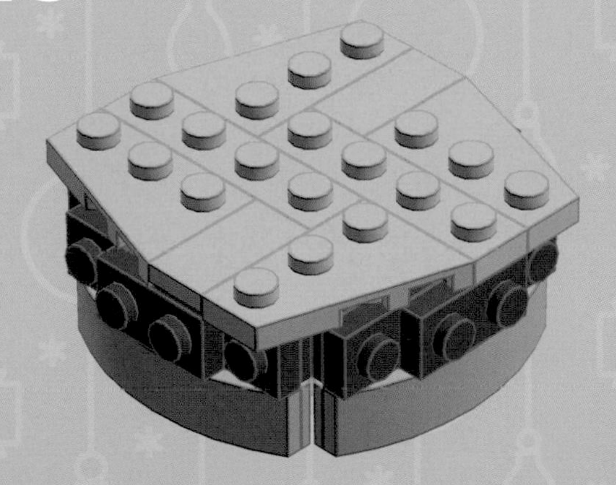

14

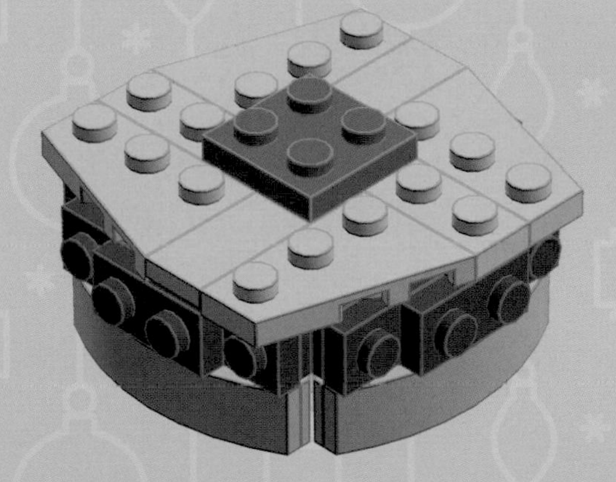

15

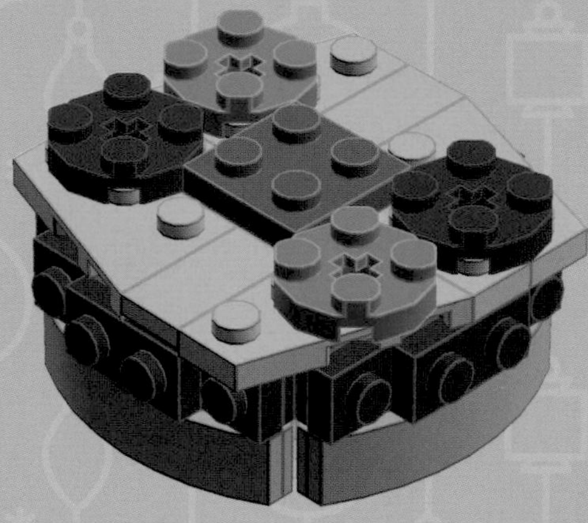

16

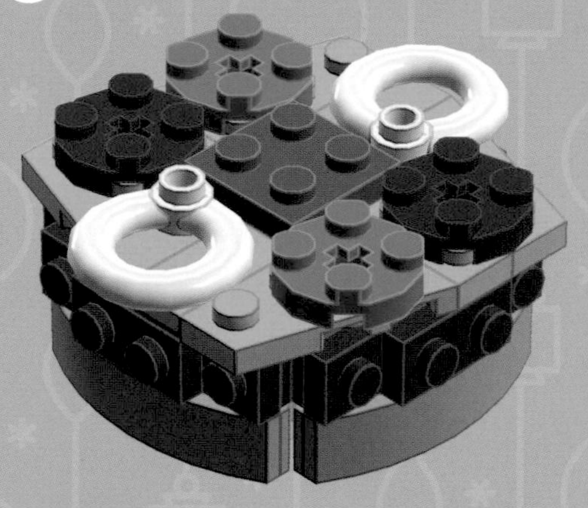

17

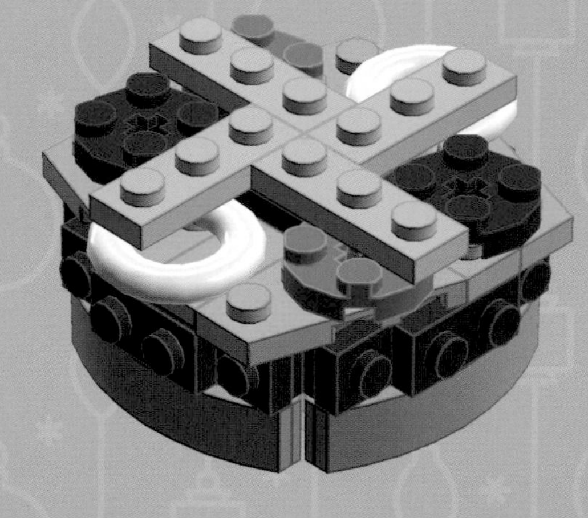

18

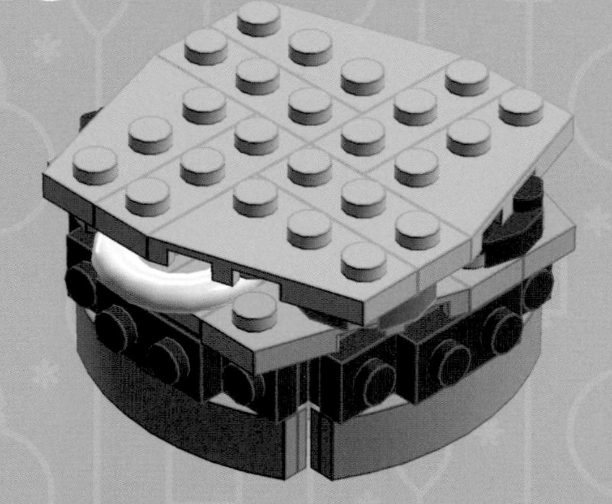

19

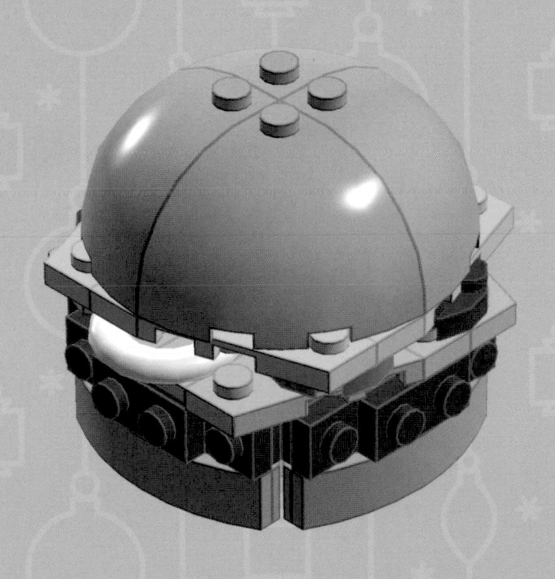

20

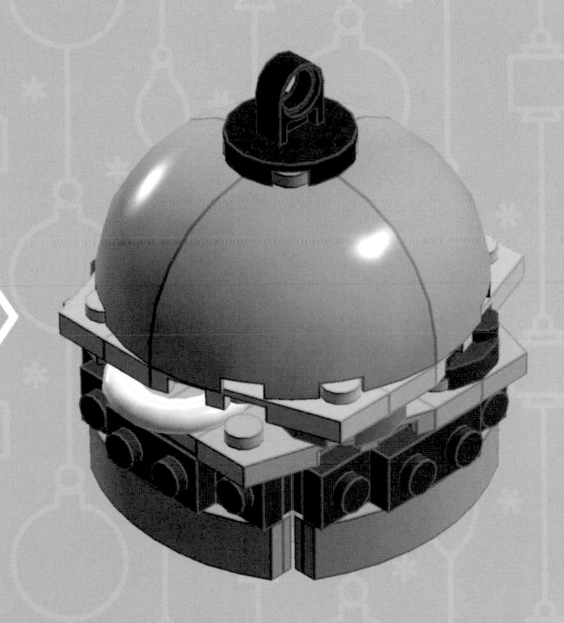

Chris McVeigh is an illustrator, photographer, and LEGO builder from Halifax, Nova Scotia. Learn more about him and his work at *chrismcveigh.com*.